Three Wounded Champions
of American Tonalism

THREE WOUNDED CHAMPIONS OF AMERICAN TONALISM

Ralph Albert Blakelock,
Homer Dodge Martin,
Alexander Helwig Wyant

Robert L. Lewis

ISBN: 1514807408
ISBN 13: 9781514807408
Library of Congress Control Number: 2015910955
CreateSpace Independent Publishing Platform
North Charleston, South Carolina

CONTENTS

ACKNOWLEDGEMENTS

At a very late stage in my life, I decided to pursue a new career, in art history, and began taking courses. I had taken a course in American abstract expressionism at CUNY Grad Center with Professor Edward Powers, a gifted teacher, but felt guilty that I knew nothing about prior American artistic endeavors. I then proceeded to take a survey course in nineteenth-century American art with Professor Kevin Avery, formerly of the Metropolitan Museum, which opened up for me the world of American landscape painting dominated by the Hudson River School. I knew the adage about how great teachers can change your life but never really experienced it before. In doing my research, I was shocked about how little has been written on the subject of certain Hudson River School artists. I only hope that my small book can bring a few of these great artists to the attention of the public.

I am indebted to the staff of the Frick Reference Library for assisting me in the use of their magnificent research facility. I wish to particularly thank Suz Massen, chief of public services, for her guidance and instruction. I have used the Watson Library at the Metropolitan Museum, the New York Historical Society Library, room 300 at the New York Public Library on 42nd Street, and the CUNY Grad Center Library. The resources at the Frick are unparalleled, and I am always amazed that they are open to any scholar who chooses to avail himself. I now live in Miami and understand more than ever what makes the Frick a world-class research facility.

I must also acknowledge my indebtedness to Dr. Jonathan Harding, curator at the Century Association. He was kind enough to give me a tour of the collection as well as to provide me with several images to use in this book. Seeing the pictures in their proper place and environment greatly heightened my understanding of their appeal and beauty. I had not known until recently that the association was still in existence and was extremely impressed with their continued role as an open storehouse for this great art.

Lastly, I have been doing my writing at the main branch of the Miami Dade Library on Flagler Avenue, in Miami, and also at the regional Miami Beach branch, across the street from the Bass Museum. Both library branches have become havens for the homeless, who seek a place of quiet where they can read and explore—by books and computer—the world from which they have become isolated. Most of us read about the "Other" but are not exposed to such people on a regular basis. In the reading rooms, the homeless are always polite and courteous and strikingly well spoken and informed. They use the bathrooms to wash and shave, while being careful to keep the facilities clean and neat. I was always led to believe that homelessness was primarily a sign of mental illness, but those I have met at the libraries seem just to have suffered one bad turn or another and cannot recover economically. Most have lost their jobs and, being in their late forties or older, cannot find replacement positions.

INTRODUCTION

Very few artistic schools end in blazes of glory; most rather gracefully decline while being replaced by new movements or styles. At present, new movements tend to develop rapidly and dissipate even quicker. The Hudson River School and the appreciation of landscape paintings by the American collecting public had a very long run, being the dominant style in American art for almost eighty years before petering out and vanishing. Nineteenth-century America is still today primarily represented by its landscape painters, with woods and fields representing historic greatness and varied emotion.

Every movement and school changes over time. Each new artist within a movement seeks to bring his individual style into the school and modify it with his own vision and approach. Given its lengthy history, the Hudson River School also underwent change, adapting to evolving needs and visions. Its final days are represented by the approaches of three wounded champions: Ralph Albert Blakelock, Homer Dodge Martin, and Alexander Helwig Wyant, each bearing his own burden and physical disability while also bringing unique insight and vision to the school. Each was damaged in a different way and each overcame his impairment, or learned to live with it, in pursuit of the production of his art. None of them would deviate from their shared goal of producing the art in which they believed.

This book is about these three artists. Ralph Albert Blakelock had emotional issues that resulted in three full breakdowns and eventually long-term confinement to a mental institution. It was only while institutionalized that he achieved recognition for his art. Homer Dodge Martin suffered from impaired vision. He could not draw a straight line and was rejected by the Union army during the Civil War because of his eyesight. Alexander Helwig Wyant suffered from poor health his entire life and had a serious stroke as a young man that paralyzed his painting hand. Undeterred, he learned to paint with his nondominant hand, succeeded in selling his paintings, and obtained many pupils. Wyant even married one of them: a young, attractive water colorist who stayed by his side until his death.

These three artists represent the final vision of the Hudson River School. In bringing their own insights, they focused on fusing various tones in their landscapes, which earned them the designation "tonalists." Today, they are at best faintly remembered; their work, slightly recognized. Time has passed them by. It is my hope that this book will bring their heroic and somewhat sad stories back to life and maybe return to them the recognition they once had.

Ralph Albert Blakelock:
Insanity, Manipulation, and Recognition with Changing Posthumous Perceptions

In the early 1900s, Ralph Albert Blakelock's expressionistic landscape paintings were in as much demand as the works of such American masters as Winslow Homer, James Whistler, and John Singer Sargent.[1] In 1916, his haunting landscape *Brook by Moonlight* (fig. 6), was sold at auction for $20,000 (equivalent to $428,000 today),[2] a record price for a painting by a living American artist. The sale, his second record price in three years, made Blakelock a celebrity. The newspapers called him America's greatest artist, while thousands flocked to exhibits of his work as a result of these unheard-of prices. As his fame blossomed, Blakelock was confined to the Middletown Psychiatric Hospital, where he had already spent the previous fifteen years. Prior to his institutionalization, he had achieved almost no recognition or success. His artistic style changed little over the course of his life. Released from the hospital, Blakelock fell into the hands of a deceitful agent, who, using the false name Beatrice Van Rensselaer Adams and having no knowledge of art, ruthlessly promoted him with great success. Blakelock achieved celebrity status on the strength of his innate talent, his artistic style having finally become

---

1 Whistler and Sargent were truly European artists who, because of heritage, are embraced as American artists. Whistler was born in Italy but went to West Point, from which he dropped out and returned to Europe. Sargent was born in Paris and lived most of his life in France and England, only living in Florida and the Caribbean late in life. Both were expatriates most of their lives, and neither painted "American" pictures.

2 All historical equivalencies ascertained through the website Measuring Worth, accessed December 9, 2014, http://www.measuringworth.com/uscompare.

popular,[3] and Adams's successfully promoting his unique and interesting story to the public.

Even when he was famous, Ralph Albert Blakelock struggled his whole life for success as a painter. He did achieve recognition, but never enough to satisfactorily provide for the material needs of his wife and nine children. In 1899, after years of teetering on the verge of emotional instability, he was committed to a mental hospital, where he more or less remained until his death in 1919. His wife and children lived nearby, in the Catskills, in dire poverty. Success and recognition only came to Blakelock after his institutionalization. Odd that his fame was further enhanced by a manipulative and fraudulent woman who used his celebrity status for her own personal advantage and obtained for herself all the financial fruits of Blakelock's success. She was careful to make use of the sensational story of his long struggle in poverty and mental breakdown to enhance the romantic image of the artist, which furthered his appeal to the general public. Blakelock and his family received nothing. Fame may come to those who sit and wait, but they may not always benefit from it.

Blakelock's painting style remained fairly constant his entire life, with his focus primarily on landscapes—some with Indian encampments, some with bright moonlight (fig. 4), others of trees and forests (fig. 7). His work was influenced by the French Barbizon tradition, and his subjective expressionist style echoes his contemporaries Albert Pinkman Ryder and George Inness.[4] Throughout his life, he did have collectors who recognized his skills and abilities, but their interest was never enough. His landscapes were too expressive, too heavily painted, and too dark for broader consumption. He did not paint what he saw but added patches of color and blurred images that expressed mood rather than replicating nature exactly. His pictures exuded the darkened foreboding of distant places. His vision of a distorted reality and use of thicker paint distinguished him from the other artists of his time

---

3 This expressionist approach to art became the successor to impressionism in both France and Germany, and evidently was at this point being appreciated in the United States. In general, the United States seemed to be about ten to twenty years behind artistic movements in Europe. This changed after World War II, with America taking the lead in artistic development.

4 Spanierman Gallery, *Ralph Albert Blakelock*, accessed November 18, 2014, http://www.spanierman.com/Blakelock.Ralph-Albert/bio/thumbs/biography.

and represented a unique view of life that was unacceptable to most collectors. Blakelock's inability to support his large family or gain recognition appears to have exacerbated his emotional issues, forcing him over the edge of insanity. I am tempted to describe him psychiatrically, but this is before Freud and would be anachronistic.[5]

During this period of chaos, many workshops were opened to copy Blakelock's paintings and to sell these forgeries as authentic works. This became a widespread practice, and even today there are still many forgeries of Blakelock's works that are being bought and sold to the public. Blakelock and his family were unable to deal with his success or to control and monitor his output.[6]

THE ARTIST PRIOR TO COMPLETE BREAKDOWN AND INSTITUTIONALIZATION

Ralph Albert Blakelock (fig. 1) was born in a tenement near the Christopher Street Wharf in Manhattan after a tremendous storm on Friday, October 15, 1847. His mother was American, but his father had arrived from England, starting out as a carpenter and then becoming a police sergeant and eventually a successful homeopathic physician. In 1864, the younger Blakelock passed the examination for admittance to the Free Academy of The City of New York, the predecessor of the College of the City of New York (now City College). He was intent on becoming a physician, like his father,[7] but dropped out in 1866 to pursue a career as an artist.[8] He was successful as a very young artist: at the age of only twenty he exhibited at the fall 1867 Exhibition of the National Academy of Design, which required the approval of a distinguished

---

5 Glyn Vincent, *The Unknown Night: The Genius and Madness of R. A. Blakelock, an American Painter* (New York: Grove, 2003), 228–97.

6 Norman A. Geske, *Beyond Madness: The Art of Ralph Blakelock, 1847–1919* (Lincoln: University of Nebraska Press, 2007), 99–103.

7 His father was also named Ralph, the twelfth in a line of English physicians from Yorkshire all named Ralph.

8 Margarita Karasoulas, *Ralph Albert Blakelock (1847–1919): Iconic Nineteenth-Century American Landscape Painter*, accessed November 18, 2014, http//www.questroyalfineart.com/artist/ralph-albert-blakelock.

selection committee.[9] Blakelock came from a humble but striving family and at an early age was on his way to achieving success as an artist.

At that time, almost all of America's distinguished artists had gone to Europe[10] to complete their training; Blakelock is among the exceptions, earning him the reputation as one of the few "authentic" American painters, which contributed to his early successes. From 1869 to 1873, he visited Kansas, Colorado, the Dakotas, Wyoming, Utah, Nevada, California, Mexico, Panama, and Jamaica. He did this in three trips: one in 1869, the second a year later in 1870, and again in 1871 after the academy's summer exhibit. It was on these trips that he sketched the Indian encampments from which he made numerous paintings over the entire course of his life.[11]

In 1873, Blakelock returned from his last trip out west, and his lifelong struggle began. He initially rented a studio on Broadway and Ninth Street, above the Vienna Bakery, with its wonderful odors. It was not luxurious, but it was just down the block from the Tenth Street Studio Building, where Winslow Homer and Albert Bierstadt had their studios. On Friday, September 19, 1873, a financial collapse occurred, causing a six-year depression that debilitated the future prospects of this budding young artist. The selection committee of the National Academy of Design rejected Blakelock in 1874, but he showed at the Brooklyn Art Association, leaving the art scene thereafter and not showing again until 1879. It is difficult enough to start a career as an artist, but a poor economy and a refusal to paint what the public wanted only worsened the situation and decreased Blakelock's chances for success. On Thursday, February 22, 1877, George Washington's birthday, he married Cora Rebecca Bailey (fig. 3), whom he had known since she was nine years old. Their first child was born in July 1877. They were a young, attractive couple with much to look forward to in life.

---

9 Vincent, *The Unknown Night*, 85–89.

10 At first they studied primarily in Düsseldorf and then Munich, but beginning in the late 1870s they started migrating to Paris and its neighboring communities.

11 Vincent, *The Unknown Night*, 93–107.

Blakelock continued as an artist and he had two pictures included in the annual spring exhibition of the National Academy of Design. Although twenty-one newspapers and magazines covered the show, Blakelock was completely ignored because he did not paint what the critics wished to see. He continued showing and was included in three exhibitions in 1880, and again in 1883. By 1882, his paintings were hanging on the walls of the Metropolitan Museum of Art and had been bought by Thomas B. Clarke, the most important collector of American art at the time. By then Blakelock had moved to East Orange, New Jersey, and taken a job in Newark painting decorative panels for an art factory. A lack of patronage and collectors of his art caused a tremendous financial strain and many times, he and his growing family—eventually nine children—lived in abject poverty.[12] Cora Blakelock described her married life as "one constant struggle with poverty, because it was absolutely impossible for Mr. Blakelock to sell his pictures, for the reason that nobody wanted them."[13]

Financial pressure and artistic failure were too much for Blakelock, and he suffered his first nervous breakdown in 1891, from which he recovered. He had a second breakdown, linked to schizophrenia and depression, in December 1898, while his wife was pregnant. His third breakdown was on September 12, 1899, with the birth of his youngest child; this time, he was taken away because the doctors felt it was unsafe to have him at home. For one thing, he had a tendency to walk around the house while brandishing a sword at his wife and children. Blakelock had tried to sell some pictures to a collector to pay for the arrival of the youngest baby but was only offered half their value. When he failed to find any other buyers, he came back to the same collector and was offered even less. He was first taken to Long Island State Hospital in the Flatbush section of Brooklyn and then transferred on June 25, 1901, to a long-term care facility, the Middletown State Homeopathic Hospital for the Insane in Middletown, New York. During his dementia, Blakelock always saw

---

12 Ibid., 128–75.

13 Cora Blakelock, foreword to *Catalogue of the Works of R. A. Blakelock and of His Daughter Marian Blakelock Exhibited at Young's Art Galleries from April 27 to May 13, 1916* (Chicago: Young's Art Galleries, 1916).

himself as fabulously wealthy. He would paint million-dollar bills and give them to friends.[14]

AFTER MENTAL BREAKDOWN AND INSTITUTIONALIZATION

Under these dire circumstances, in a long-term mental care facility, Blakelock began to achieve success. Five months after being sent to Middletown, his work was selected in February 1900 for inclusion in the American exhibit of art at the Universal Exposition in Paris. Blakelock was chosen in part because he represented a true American artist: one trained in the United States and painting pictures of American scenes. The panel that selected Blakelock included William Merritt Chase, Winslow Homer, and John LaFarge, the most distinguished American artists of the time. In December 1900, William T. Evans, a long-time patron and collector, loaned his collection to the Lotos Club, and Blakelock had his first one-man exhibition. In 1902, a corrupt New York City politician named Frederick S. Gibbs, who understood publicity and promotion, bought seventy-six Blakelocks, published a catalogue, and exhibited the paintings, again, at the Lotos Club. In 1903, three important galleries, Knoedler and Macbeth in New York and Vose in Boston, began exhibiting his work. Paintings that Blakelock had sold for fifty dollars were now sold for five hundred. In 1904, *The Pipe Dance* (fig. 5) sold for $3,100 (equivalent to about $83,700 in 2014 dollars).[15]

This did not last, and by 1905 Blakelock was, for the most part, forgotten again. Few knew he was in an asylum or even alive, but several artists and collectors still admired him. In 1913, Senator William A. Clark, one of the richest men in America, bought *Moonlight* at auction for $13,900 (roughly $337,000 in 2014 dollars). In 1916 *Brook by Moonlight* (fig. 6) was purchased by Edmund Drummond Libbey for $20,000 (about $438,000) and donated to the Toledo Museum, the highest price ever paid for a painting by a living

---

14 Lloyd Goodrich, "Ralph Albert Blakelock," in *Ralph Albert Blakelock Centenary Exhibition* (New York: Whitney Museum of American Art, 1947).

15 Ibid., 32.

American artist. Money does talk, and with these high prices, Blakelock, in 1914, was finally elected an associate of the American Academy of Design in 1914. Two years later, he was elected a full academician.[16] By then he was an old, beaten man (fig. 2).

Meanwhile, Cora Blakelock and her nine children remained in abject poverty. They left their home on Atlantic Avenue in Brooklyn and moved to the dying rural town in Catskill, New York, which was near the asylum and was less expensive than Brooklyn. Blakelock's daughter, Marian, was an artist[17] but suffered a mental breakdown in 1915 and was institutionalized at the Hudson River State Hospital. At that time, Cora had not visited her husband in three years because she did not have the money for transportation.

A year later, in 1916, a young reporter from *The World* personally visited Cora and invited her, all expenses paid, to come to New York and meet Beatrice Van Rensselaer Adams, which she did on March 17, 1916. Adams explained that she wished to help the family with the establishment of the Blakelock Fund, and they proceeded to visit Ralph at Middletown in a touching reunion for the public to see. There was even a photo session and much talk about his substantial improvement[18]—all done to heighten his celebrity and make him better known to the collecting public. This was the only publicity he received, and without it his status would have languished, perhaps even disappearing from the public eye entirely.

On Tuesday, April 11, 1916, the sixty-eight-year-old Blakelock, all dressed up (fig. 2), was taken by Adams and Dr. Ashley of the asylum to Manhattan, where he appeared at the opening of an exhibit at the prestigious Reinhardt Galleries featuring forty-three of his paintings. The room was full of journalists, but neither his wife nor his children were present. From there he had his portrait professionally taken, went to a banquet lunch at the Woodstock Hotel, and made appearances at a smaller exhibition at Knoedler Gallery and then

---

16 Ibid., 35.

17 Her paintings are still collected and occasionally come up for auction. It is said that she would paint in her father's style and then sign his name to the paintings so that she could sell them as his and obtain much-needed money.

18 Vincent, *The Unknown Night*, 228–46.

the Metropolitan Museum of Art. From there, Adams took him to Grand Central Station and sent him back to Middletown in the care of Ashley. Five days later, the Reinhardt Gallery announced that 2,518 visitors had each paid a dollar (equivalent to a total of $55,100 in 2014 dollars) to see the exhibition. Personal appearances and publicity do heighten celebrity status, and people wish to be exposed to it.

Adams successfully controlled and manipulated Blakelock, obtaining all the benefits of his fame and celebrity, which she used for her own purposes. All told, it is estimated that she raised a total of $35,000 (equivalent to $766,000)[19] for the Blakelock Fund, none of which went to the artist or his family. When the family sought to discover the truth, Adams would move Blakelock around from place to place, keeping him hidden and a total prisoner until his death.[20]

BEATRICE VAN RENSSELAER ADAMS

Adams was a total fabrication. Born as Sadie Filbert in 1884, she hailed from Fishkill, New York. She left home at sixteen and married an imposter, "Louis Adams," which was but one of his names, at age eighteen. She, her husband, and their two children traveled the country committing scams until he was arrested in Chicago in 1906. He promptly posted bail and fled. Eventually caught, he went to jail; Sadie Filbert, twenty-three at the time, placed both children in an Albany orphanage and went to Chicago. By 1909, she was back in New York, with her new name Beatrice Van Rensselaer Adams to signify wealth and American aristocracy.

At this point, Adams discovered the world of nonprofit fundraising. Starting with Lincoln Memorial College in Cumberland Gap, Tennessee, established for the education of poor women and children, she proceeded to raise money for southern educational institutions. After a relentless letter-writing campaign to President Woodrow Wilson, she was appointed a representative to the National Child Labor Committee Annual Conference in

---

19 Ibid.
20 Ibid., 249–53.

New Orleans. This endeavor collapsed in 1915, and while visiting a friend in Catskill during that summer learned about Cora Blakelock. With the sale of Blakelock's *Brook by Moonlight* (fig. 6) for $20,000 in 1916, Adams knew her new mission.

Adams found a friend in Middletown Hospital's physician Ashley, who adored sharp suits, powerful cars and understood public relations. He accompanied her all over, and may have had a personal interest in her as well. Slowly Adams won him over in support of Blakelock's parole from the hospital. Blakelock even died in the custody of Adams, at an Adirondack camp on August 14, 1919.[21]

In 1924 Adams moved to a home in Leeds, New York, next door to the farm where Cora Blakelock was living, but they never spoke. Adams tried to raise money to write a biography of Blakelock but then disappeared. On December 23, 1941, while ranting about Blakelock, she collapsed near Grand Central Station, just steps from an exhibition of his work at Grand Central Galleries. She was taken to King's Park State Hospital and diagnosed with paranoid schizophrenia. She spoke the whole time of what she had done on behalf of Blakelock and how she was a woman of great means. Her medical chart indicates that, even four years after her admission, she never received a single letter or visitor. The persona she had used to generate publicity for Blakelock also affected her, as she had assumed many of the same delusions as Blakelock, while apparently becoming his biggest fan.

THE ART

Blakelock had separated himself from the strictures of the academy and sought an alternative view of the painter's relationship to his environment. He started painting in the style of the Hudson River School but bypassed luminism for the French Barbizon school and expressionism. He never visited Europe, so we can only speculate on his influences. He did have an opportunity to see European art at public exhibitions, and his friend and dealer Seth

---

21 Goodrich, "Ralph Albert Blakelock," 41.

Vose, in Boston, was exhibiting Barbizon paintings as early as 1852.[22] He is also compared to a few contemporaneous artists, such as Homer Dodge Martin and Alexander Helwig Wyant of the American Barbizon School and Albert Pinkham Ryder, a unique expressionist. But in truth, Blakelock's works are very distinct. This difference in style from mainstream American art held back his career. He could only obtain fame and recognition once the viewing public had acclimated themselves to his form of art. By the early 1880s, postimpressionism and expressionism began appearing in Europe and, with a lag, probably became recognized and accepted in America by the late 1890s.

It took Blakelock many years to gain recognition because his work was so different that the American viewing public could not appreciate or even accept it. The first European expressionists were Van Gogh and Gauguin, and this was first in 1890. It is reasonable to estimate that American collectors were not exposed to European impressionism until 1900, when Blakelock began to experience fame. Blakelock's work is reminiscent of the student who skips a few grades: he was ahead of his time. He had to wait for his viewing public to accept his vision.

Eventually, his style was recognized by the American press as a Romantic painter similar to Turner or as a Barbizon painter similar to Rousseau because the media did not really know how to describe his work or peers.[23] Blakelock painted dark, diffused landscapes, sometimes with single rays of light shining through them, as in his famous *Moonlight* paintings (e.g., fig. 4). George Inness, an American Barbizon painter, did similar work toward the end of his life but was fortunate enough to have obtained recognition in his early years so that he had the freedom to paint as he chose when he grew older. By the time Blakelock's work was being appreciated, other artists had already independently acquired his style and even moved forward with it. In many ways, O'Keeffe's work is an extension of Blakelock, with more abstraction and softer, lighter colors.

---

22 Geske, *Beyond Madness*, 8–12.

23 *Boston Evening Transcript*, "One of Blakelock's Masterly Nocturnes," February 20, 1917.

TALENT AND PROMOTION CONTRIBUTING
TO BLAKELOCK'S FAME

It is a mixture of time, talent, and promotion that produces a celebrity. It was unfortunate that Blakelock received his share of stardom when it was already too late and he was beyond repair. It is tragic that his talent and story were publicized by a ruthless person seeking to use it for her own financial advantage. Turner[24] defines three processes that produce a celebrity: (1) a culture that privileges the momentary, visual, and sensational; (2) the consumers of celebrity recognizing it as an innate or natural quality possessed by extraordinary individuals; and (3) certain economic processes. These all applied to Blakelock, a starving artist ahead of his time and committed to a mental asylum. This was the fertile material that Beatrice Van Rensselaer Adams knew to promote. She had a story to tell that would be attractive to the collecting public, hungry for sensationalism. Blakelock's star was already on the ascent in the sense that he had a compelling tale and, after a point, recognized talent.

Writing about his grandfather in the 1970s, David Blakelock believed that no other American artist received more publicity in newspapers and magazines at any time than Blakelock received from 1916 to 1919, and particularly in 1916, when Adams was at her height. He says that this massive publicity greatly hurt his relatives because it focused primarily on "his poor destitute family" and because "his mental illness was greatly over-emphasized."[25] This was exactly what the public wished to read and what added to his celebrity status.

Turner[26] links the development of celebrity with the growth of mass media, in particular visual media, which began in the period between 1895 and 1920, when it became possible to mass-produce visual images cheaply. The press needed something that could provide the public with a supply of sensations and real-life adventure. It was during this time period that Adams succeeded in promoting Blakelock as a celebrity. Even with her great efforts, his

---

24 Graham Turner, *Understanding Celebrity* (London: Sage, 2004), 4.

25 David A. Blakelock, *Ralph Albert Blakelock* (New York: M. Knoedler, 1973), 20.

26 Ibid., 10.

star only rose momentarily, and within a few years he was all but forgotten. Adams was able to keep his momentum alive a little longer, and it probably would have faded sooner without her.

The great German essayist Walter Benjamin[27] discusses how the early nineteenth century produced a crisis in painting because, with rising incomes and education, the medium became part of a simultaneous collective experience, where once it had been a more individual experience for the select few who could actually view such images. This crisis, requiring painting to become something more than faithful realism, was not caused exclusively by the development of photography but by the appeal of artwork to the masses. Paintings, which had previously been the exclusive domain of the critical few, were now enjoyed by the masses. It was precisely at this time that Blakelock began to achieve recognition because his work was not simply an accurate portrayal of landscape but incorporated his personal feelings and expressed his private thoughts. His paintings appealed to and attracted the attention of the newly educated and affluent who sought to widen their cultural experiences.

The film studies scholar Richard Dyer makes much of the concept of "stars compensating people for qualities lacking in their lives."[28] This idea helps to explain why Blakelock, who was the underdog, the rejected, the failure, finally succeeded and made good for himself. Consumers could identify with not being recognized for their special skills and for life passing them by. If Blakelock could finally succeed, there was hope for them as well. This is a powerful concept that still exists with us today: the peasant rising to lead the king's armies to victory or the shoeshine boy becoming a millionaire. Blakelock was the classic tale of the great starving artist who is finally discovered and recognized. Sadly, it was only fleeting and even and even at its zenith, could not be fully appreciated by him.

---

27 Walter Benjamin, "The Work of Art in the Age of Mechanical Reproduction," in *Stardom and Celebrity: A Reader*, ed. Sean Redmond and Sue Holmes (London: Sage, 2007), 25–33.
28 Richard Dyer, "Stars," in *Stardom and Celebrity: A Reader*, ed. Sean Redmond and Sue Holmes (London: Sage, 2007), 81.

Posthumous Aftermath

I would now wish to examine Blakelock's paintings in the aftermath of his brief encounter with fame. Thirty years is sufficient time for a new generation of collectors, critics, and scholars to come on the scene, so his status as an artist will be studied from the thirtieth anniversary of the sale of *Brook by Moonlight* (fig. 6) in 1946 to the present. Although pricing does reflect some measure of value and recognition, newspaper and magazine articles, exhibitions and scholarly mentions matter, too. Newspaper articles are sourced primarily from the ProQuest Historical Newspapers database. Pricing from 1946 to 1984 is based on *World Collectors Annuary*,[29] and on ArtNet from 1986 to 2014.[30] As referred to and cited previously, the *BioBibliography: An Annotated Chronology of the Life of Ralph Albert Blakelock*, as established by Norman A. Geske of the University of Nebraska in *Beyond Madness*,[31] provides a framework.

The pricing history shows much divergence primarily because of the numerous fakes and forgeries created of Blakelock's paintings during his brief period of fame during his lifetime and immediately after his death in 1919. As late as 1928, Harry W. Watrous, a benefactor of Blakelock who had his studio nearby and a vice-president of the National Academy of Design, had examined fifty pictures allegedly by Blakelock. Watrous stated in an interview that "he could not assert that more than 10 per cent were genuine. Another 10 percent came within the doubtful class, which could not be stamped forgeries with complete assurance. The remained obviously were forged."[32]

The Nebraska Catalogue Inventory has made great efforts to clarify this situation but does not regard itself as a catalogue raisonné. Many auction records antedate the Nebraska Catalogue Inventory, and many of those thereafter do not refer to their classification. In evaluating pricing trends, it has been assumed that those paintings fetching higher prices have a provenance

---

29 A. M. E. Van Eijk Van Voorthusijsen, ed., *World Collectors Annuary* (Delft, Netherlands: Brouwer, n.d.).

30 Artnet price database, accessed December 23, 2014, http://www.artnet.com/PDB/FAADsearch/FAADResults3.aspx?page=1&ArtType=F.

31 Geske, *Beyond Madness*, 113–50.

32 "Fake Blakelocks Flood Art Market," *New York Times*, January 20, 1928.

more proved than those selling at substantially lower prices, although it does appear that the size of the painting can be an important consideration. For ease of comparison, equivalent current prices have been provided within parentheses.[33] Where more than five paintings were sold at auction in any year, the highest price and then the range of high and low prices for the remainder are listed. There are large time gaps, perhaps due to a lack of auction sales or simple clerical omissions.

1946

Landscape with Figures, 15 ½ × 26" Collection of Dr. M.C. Gould, New York, 1916, at Parke Bernet New York 5/1/46 $120 ($1,430).

The White Captive, 14 × 22" Collection of M.C. Gould, New York, 1916, at Parke Bernet New York $140 ($1,670).

Old New York, 16 ¼ × 24" From the C.W. Kraushaar Galleries, New York, Collection of Dr. Arthur P. Coll, New York, 1922 at Parke Bernet New York $500 ($5,960).

The Return of the Hunter, 25 × 29 ½" From Robert C. Vose, Boston 1926, Parke Bernet New York $475 ($5,660).

Sunset, 22 × 47" From Henry W. Ranger, New York 1916, Parke Bernet New York $350 ($4,170)

1947

Landscape with Indians at Sunset, 4 × 5" Parke Bernet New York $100 ($1,040).

Going to the Spring, 8 × 51/2" from Charles M. Kurtz, Buffalo, Parke Bernet New York $170 ($1,770).

Moonlight Waters, 13 ½ × 18", Parke Bernet New York $200 ($2,090).

The Necklace, 29 × 26", Parke Bernet New York $1,700 ($17,700)

A large single artist exhibition was held at the Whitney Museum of American Art, commemorating the hundredth anniversary of Blakelock's birth and

---

33 Measuring Worth, accessed January 7, 2015, http://www.measuringworth.com/uscompare.

of the City College of New York.[34] A very impressive catalogue by Lloyd Goodrich, cited previously, and numerous reviews. Blakelock was the selected for this exhibition because he had attended City College in its first incarnation. It seems that the showing made little difference to the collecting public, with scant sales at lower prices continuing. Several favorable reviews were written about the exhibition. The higher price obtained for *The Necklace* can perhaps be attributed to the exhibition.

1948

Autumn Landscape, (signed initials only), 5 × 11 1/2", Parke Bernet New York $25 ($242).
Cloudy Morning, 12 × 30, from William Macbeth Galleries, New York, Parke Bernet New York $175 ($1,690).

1949

Out of the Deepening Shadows, 8 × 12 ½", Parke Bernet New York $225 ($2,200).

1950

Near Clivedale, 12 × 17", From Thomas B. Clarke, New York, Parke Bernet New York $80 ($774).
Indian Encampment, 17 × 21", (Certificate of Authenticity from Harry w. Watrous and Elliott Daingerfield) Parke Bernet New York $300 ($2,900).
Golden Twilight, 13 ½ × 9", Parke Bernet New York $100 ($967).

1951

Evening Landscape, 22 ¼ × 42", Parke Bernet New York $500 ($4,480).

---

34 Edward Allen Jewell, 100th Anniversary of Blakelock's Birth Is Marked by Exhibition at the Whitney," *New York Times*, April 22, 1947, 32.

1963

Autumn Landscape with a Fisherman, 12 × 22", From Langenbach, Parke Bernet New York $1,900 ($14,500).

1964

Indian Encampment Late Evening, 10 × 11", From A.C. Baker, Newark, N.J., Parke Bernet New York $700 ($5,260).

1965

Solitude, 10 × 11", From Elizabeth Molnar, Parke Bernet New York $1000 ($7,610).

Afterglow, 16 ¾ × 24 ½", From Elizabeth Molnar (with a detailed and complete provenance), Parke Bernet New York $1,500 ($11,400).

1966

Autumn Landscape with a Fisherman, 12 × 22" (sold previously on 9/10/63 for $1,900), Parke Bernet New York $1,400 ($10,000).

1967

Landscape with Indians, 7 ¼ × 4 1/8", Parke Bernet New York $975 ($6,800).

1971

Hunter and Dog, 27 × 22", From Macbeth Gallery, New York, Parke Bernet New York $9,000 ($51,800).

An Opening in the Woods, 24 ¼ × 16 ¾" (impeccable and impressive provenance) Parke Bernet New York $4,500 ($25,900).

Landscape with Cattle, 6 × 12", (Nebraska Inventory Number [but no category]) Parke Bernet New York $1,600 ($9,200).

Landscape, 6 × 12", From William Schaus, New York, (Nebraska Inventory Number [but no category]) Parke Bernet New York $3000 ($17,300).

1972

The Pond, 5 ½ × 9 ¼ From Knoedler, New York, Parke Bernet New York $2,700 ($15,000).

Deepening Shadows, 16 × 22 ¼", From Vose, Boston (Nebraska Inventory Number [but no category]) Parke Bernet $7,500 ($41,700).

Cloudy Morning, Camp Niddick, Maine, 12 × 20" (sold previously in 1948 for $175) Parke Bernet New York $3,500 ($19,500).

Indian Encampment, 9 × 11", From Grand Central Art galleries, New York, Parke bernet new York $3,300 ($18,400).

The Farm Yard, 6 × 8", From Vose, Boston (Exhibited Worchester Museum and J.W. Young Gallery, Chicago) Parke Bernet New York $4,000 ($22,300).

1973

Woodland Stream, 23 ½ × 39 ½", Parke Bernet New York $7,750 ($40,600).

Indian and Tepee on a Lake, 10 ½ × 16 ¼", Sotheby's Parke Bernet New York $3,700 ($19,400)

Landscape at Sunset, 18 × 27.5 cm, Parke Bernet New York $1,800 ($9,430)

Wooded Landscape, 30.5 × 36 cm, Park Bernet New York $1,800 (9,430)

1976

The Old Mill, 68.6 × 55.9 cm (Exhibited M. Knoedler, New York 1973, University of Nebraska Art Galleries, Lincoln 1975, New Jersey State Museum, Trenton 1975) Parke Bernet New York $5,250 ($21,500).

This exhibition was organized by the University of Nebraska and also exhibited in Trenton. It included approximately one hundred oil paintings, drawings, and sketches.[35] It received favorable reviews but still had little effect

---

35 Piri Halasz, "Art by Blakelock Shown in Trenton," *New York Times*, May 18, 1975, NJ83.

upon Blakelock's market, although it may have produced the higher price obtained for *The Old Mill.*

1977

Farm Scene, 18 × 32", From Judge Norman S. Dike, New York, Acquired from the Artist ca. 1887, Parke Bernet New York $3,000 ($11,500)

1980

Mountain Lake, 21 × 39 ¼", Parke Bernet New York $20,000 ($56,600)
In 1978 by Abraham A. Davidson published a book in which Blakelock is highly regarded and compared to Albert Pinkham Ryder, and his artistic style linked to the French Barbizon painters.[36]

1984

Indian Encampment, 5 ½ × 9 ½", Christie's New York $5,280 ($11,800)

1986

Indian Encampment, 11.8 × 17.9", Christie's New York $5,500 ($11,700)

1987

Morning Road, 8 × 10", Sotheby's Arcade New York $1,760 ($3,610)
Indian Encampment, 8.3 × 12.1", Christie's New York $3,850 ($7,900)
Morning, Indian Encampment, 22 × 44.5", Sotheby's New York $26,400 ($54,100)
A major exhibition of forty-six of his canvases was held at Salander-O'Reilly Galleries and received favorable reviews. It was the first exhibition of his paintings in New York since 1973 and the largest since Blakelock's centenary

36 Abraham A. Davidson, *The Eccentrics and Other American Visionary Painters* (New York: E. P. Dutton, 1978), 144–50.

exhibition at the Whitney Museum of American Art.[37] It seems to have had little effect upon his prices and sales, except maybe for the higher price obtained by *Morning, Indian Encampment.*

1989

Pioneer Home, 17 × 33", Sotheby's Arcade $5,500 ($10,300)
Enchanted Pool, 29 × 36", Sotheby's New York $49,500 ($93,000)
Evening Landscape, 16 × 24", Sotheby's Arcade $6,600 ($12,400)
Landscape with Indians, 20 × 30", Christie's East $2,860 ($5,370)

1990

Sunset in Autumn Landscape, 6.3 × 9.4", Butterfields $3,300 ($5,880)
Landscape, 7.8 × 11.8", Sotheby's Arcade $3,300 ($5,880)
A Woodland Stream, 8.1 × 5.7", Christie's New York $3,850 ($6,860)
Twilight Mood, 16.1 × 24.1", Christie's New York $4,950 ($8,820)
Fall landscape with Stream and Distant Hills, 18 × 31.7", Christie's East $2,750 ($4,900)

1991

Meadow, Middleton, New York, 5.1 × 10", Butterfields $4,675 ($8,000)
Autumn Landscape, 8.1 × 5.6", Christie's New York $3,080 ($5,270)
Middletown Landscape, 5.5 × 8.5", Christie's New York $7,700 ($13,200)
Indian Woman by Stream, 16.1 × 23.9", Christie's New York $4,400 ($7,530)
Indian Encampment in the Woods, 8.5 × 12.6", Christie's New York $3,520 ($6,020)

1992

Landscape Twilight, 4.5 × 5.5", Christie's New York $3,520 ($5,840)

---

37 Roberta Smith, "Art: The Landscapes of Ralph A. Blakelock," *New York Times*, September 11, 1987, C26.

Indian Encampment, 5.9 × 8.1", Christie's East $3,450 ($5,730)
A Mountain Watershed, 18 × 32", Sotheby's New York $14,300 ($23,700)
Walking Along the River, 27 × 35", Butterfields $7,150 ($11,900)

1993

Deep Woods, 37 × 21.5", Sotheby's New York $17,250 ($27,800)
Landscape with Clouds, 4.5 × 7", Christie's New York $1,500 ($2,420)
The Old Mill, 18 × 32, Christie's New York $6,325 ($10,200)
Teepees in the Moonlight, 27.1 × 23, Christie's New York $55,200 ($89,000)
Jamaican Coastal Scene, 35 × 56", Sotheby's New York $76,750 ($124,000)

1994

The Canoe Builders, 13.2 × 11.8", Christie's New York $43,700 ($68,700)
Another six paintings were sold that year ranging in price from $2,300 ($3,620) to $10,950 ($17,200).

1995

Indian Encampment in Daylight, 16 × 24", Doyle New York $6,612 ($10,100)
Another seven paintings were sold that year ranging in price from $1,700 ($2,600) to $4,400 ($6,730).

1997

Twilight Landscape, 7.1 × 12", Sotheby's New York $2,875 ($4,170)
Moonlit Landscape, 8.2 × 6", Mystic Fine Arts $2,352 ($3,410)
Civil War Soldier in his Tent, 10.8 × 8", Mystic Fine Art $3,024 ($4,390)
Moonlit Landscape, 14 × 20", Sotheby's Arcade $4,312 ($6,260)
Indian Encampment at Dusk, 11.5 × 16", Grogan & Company $2,645 ($3,840)
During 1996, Abraham A. Davidson (whose book is previously cited and mentioned) of the Council for Creative Projects, organized a traveling

exhibition containing more than forty of Blakelock's works that he created while institutionalized.[38] The exhibition was shown at the Heckscher Museum in Huntington, Long Island from March to April 7, 1997.[39] It received good reviews but seems to have had no effect on the market for the artist's work.

1998

Autumn in the Adirondacks, 18 × 32, Christie's New York $11,500 ($16,400)
Indian Encampment at Sunset, 18 × 25", Sotheby's Arcade $$3,450 ($4,930)
Indian Encampment, 21 × 37", Doyle New York $3,220 ($4,600)
Indian Hunting, 21 × 29", Doyle New York $2,760 ($3,940)
Jamaican Coastal Scene, 35 × 56", Sotheby's New York $101,500 ($145,000)

1999

Nocturne with Full Moon, 10 × 14", Coeur d'Alene Auction $15,400 ($21,500)
Another ten paintings were sold that year ranging in price from $6,500 ($9,090) to $1,955 ($2,730).

2000

Indian Encampment along the Snake River, 47.5 × 84", Sotheby's New York $3,525,750 ($4,770,000)
Another eight paintings were sold that year ranging in price from $302,750 ($410,000) to $4,025 ($5,450).
This is by far the highest price ever achieved by any of Blakelock's paintings. It is almost an aberration, and the reason for this price has not been discovered.

---

38 Helen A. Harrison, "A Visionary Artist's Output During a Time of Mental Illness," *New York Times*, March 3, 1996, L116.

39 Roberta Smith, "Islands of Peace in a Life Awash in Sadness," *New York Times*, March 17, 1996, H45.

2001
View of a Cottage with Cows Watering, 12 × 20.2", Christie's East $3,760 ($4,950)
Woodland Stream, 7.1 × 4.6", Skinner $4,888 ($6,430)
Moonlight, 16.7 × 14", Sotheby's New York $9,000 ($11,800)
Stingtown Pike, 9.8 × 13", Shannon's $6,900 ($9,080)

2002
Sunset Over Mountains, 20 × 12", Christies New York $31,070 ($40,200)
Another twelve paintings were sold that year. ranging in price from $14,340 ($18,600) to $1,955 ($2,530). It should be noted that auction sales occurred at Gros & Delettrez, Paris, and at Phillips, de Pury & Luxembourg, New York, a more contemporary auction house.

2003
Indian Camp, 16.5 × 24.5", Sotheby's New York $78,000 ($98,800)
Another nine paintings were sold that year, ranging in price from $66,000 ($83,600) to $1,550 ($1,960).

2004
Indian Encampment, 8.5 × 12", Coeur d'Alene Art Auction $30,240 ($37,300)
Another seventeen paintings were sold that year, ranging in price from $26,888 ($33,200) to 2,390 ($2,950). The auction house obtaining the highest price is known for its specialization in western American art.

2005
Moonlight, 25 × 30", Christie's New York $28,800 ($34,400)
Another nine paintings sold that year, ranging in price from $22,800 ($27,200) to $3,000 ($3,580). Please note that the second-highest sales price was obtained at Christie's Los Angeles in a sale of western and American paintings.

2006

California Red Woods, 18 × 32", Sotheby's New York $33,000 ($38,100)
Another six pictures were sold that year, ranging in price from $20,400 ($23,600) to $4,750 ($5,490).

2007

Encampment on the Upper Missouri, 26 × 36", Coeur d'Alene Art Auction $201,600 ($227,000)
Another six paintings were sold that year, ranging in price from $18,000 ($20,200) to $11,875 ($13,300).
Norman A. Geske of The University of Nebraska, published his definitive book on Blakelock in 2007, but with little or no effect on the market for the artist's paintings.

2008

Moonlight, 18.5 × 26", Christie's New York $30,000 ($32,500)
Another eight paintings were sold that year, ranging in price from $20,000 ($21,600) to $1,500 ($1,620). One picture was sold at the German auction house Van Ham Kunstauktionen.

2009

Landscape, 12 × 18", Leslie Hindman Auctioneers $30,500 ($33,100)
Another eight paintings sold that year, ranging in price from $11,875 ($12,900) to $5,100 ($5,540)

2010

Indian Encampment at Dusk, 14 × 22", Neal Auction Company $3,424 ($3,660)
Landscape at Moonlight, 16 × 22", Christie's New York $27,500 ($29,400)
Upper New York landscape with Shanties, 4 × 8.5", Bonhams New York $7,930 ($8,470)

2011

Golden Glow, 16.3 × 24.3", Christie's New York $52,500 ($54,400)
Another six paintings sold that year, ranging in price from $11,875 ($12,300) to $2,200 ($2,280)

2012

Moonlight, 12 × 20", Christie's New York $56,250 ($57,100)
Another five paintings were sold that year, ranging in price from $13,035 ($13,200) to $5,938 ($6,020). Heritage, a Dallas-based auction house specializing in western American art, sold two of the paintings.

2013

Moonlit Scene with Native American, (no dimensions) Kaminski Auctions $14,000
Another six paintings were sold that year, ranging in price from $8,024 to $1,875.

2014

Landscape, 12 × 15", DuMouchelles Fine Art Auctioneers $3,000
Wood's Edge, 8 × 11", Swann Galleries $3,500
Grey Clouds with Figures on the Hill, 10 × 18", Clars Auction Gallery $2,250
Indian Encampment, 8 × 12", Doyles New York $$6,875
Deer in Autumn Landscape, 10 ¼ × 15 1/4, Doyle New York $4,375
Encampment, 3.1 × 4.4", Freeman's $9,375

CONCLUSION

Many factors contribute to the rise and fall of artistic recognition, celebrity and fame. Sometimes only one factor is enough, but many times it is a convergence of many positive influences. These factors may not necessarily be simultaneous but may come at various times which help to continue the fame of the person. Blakelock benefited from many different factors, which were staggered but seemed to converge on him at an opportune time. Blakelock always had talent, but it simply passed unnoticed by the critics and collectors. He stayed with his concepts and lived with the rejection. With changing times and views, Blakelock's work became recognized and appreciated. It was not that Blakelock changed in any way—he was in an asylum at the time—rather, the times changed and drew him in. The story of his struggles and family poverty, as well as his mental instability, added to his fame once his work itself began to be appreciated. Prior to that time, his poverty was of little concern to anyone. The broadcasting and publicity generated by Beatrice Van Rensselaer Adams as a one-woman public relations concern did not add anything new to his life story but merely fueled the flames and succeeded in promoting Blakelock and his reputation as a gifted painter.

Even many years after his death, the prices of his paintings and his recognition seem to fluctuate randomly. Exhibitions and reviews do not seem to add any sustainability to the market for his paintings. The upswing in prices and interest in collecting nineteenth-century American art, which occurred from 1980 through 2000, may have had the most impact upon Blakelock's prices and caused the increased sales of his paintings at auction.

FIGURES

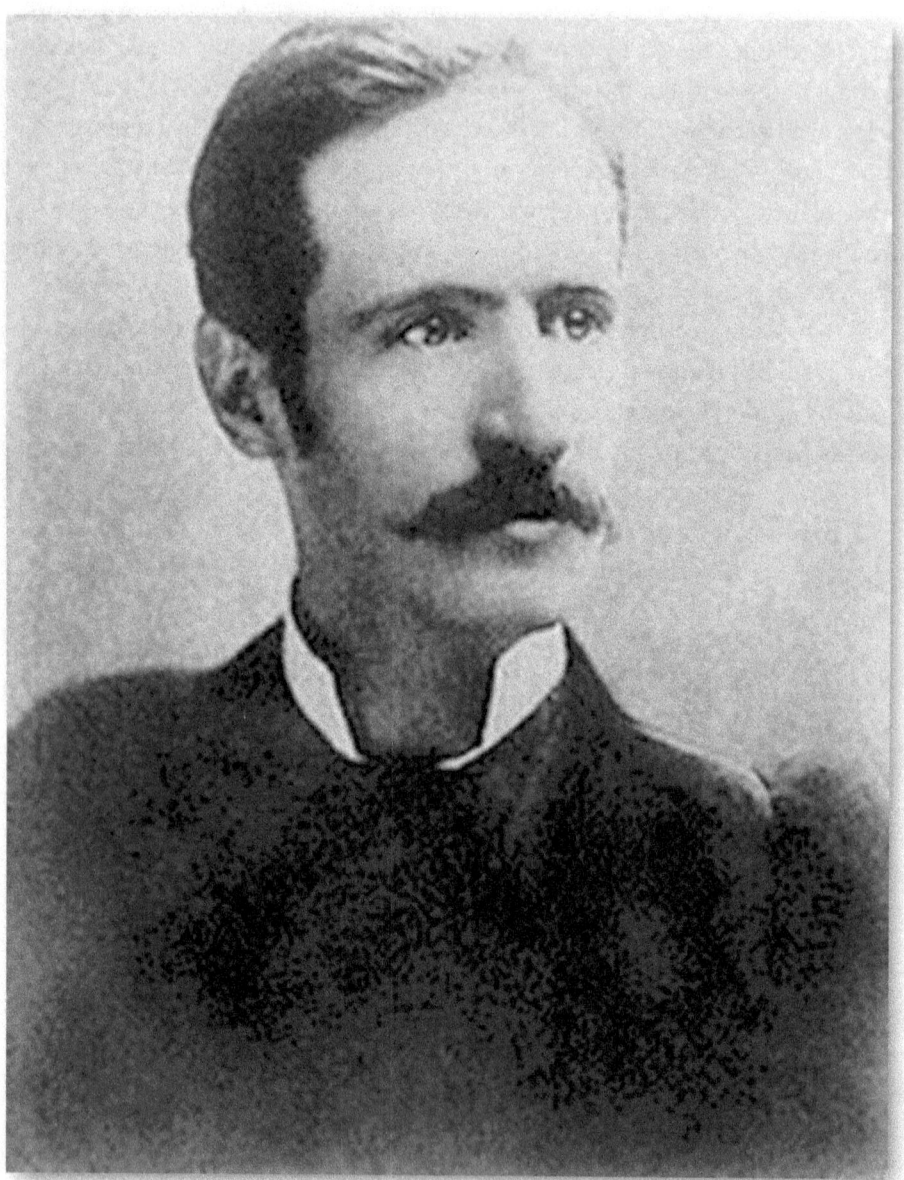

Figure 1. Ralph Albert Blakelock, ca. 1870. Black-and-white photographic print, 12 × 10 cm (photographer unknown). Smithsonian Institution, Washington, DC.

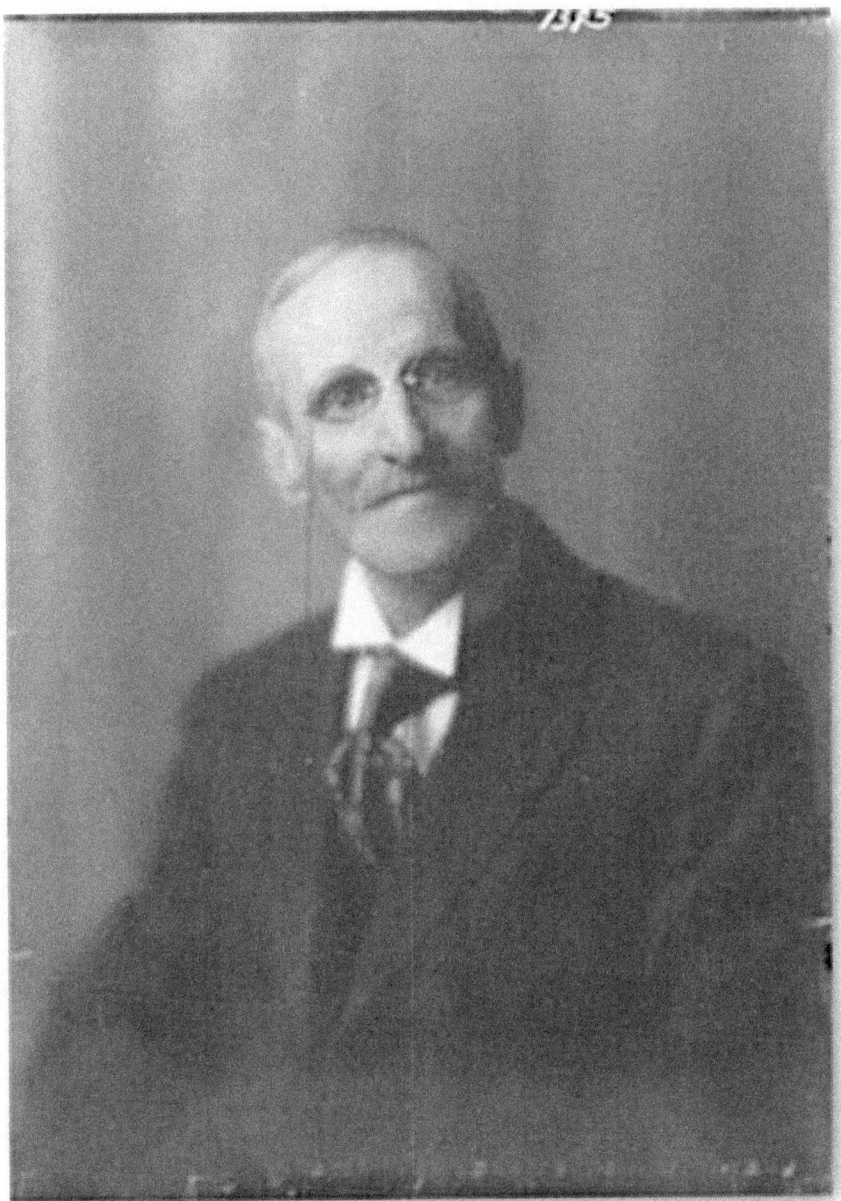

Figure 2. Ralph Albert Blakelock, April 11, 1916. Glass negative, 5 × 7 in (photographer unknown). Library of Congress, Washington, DC.

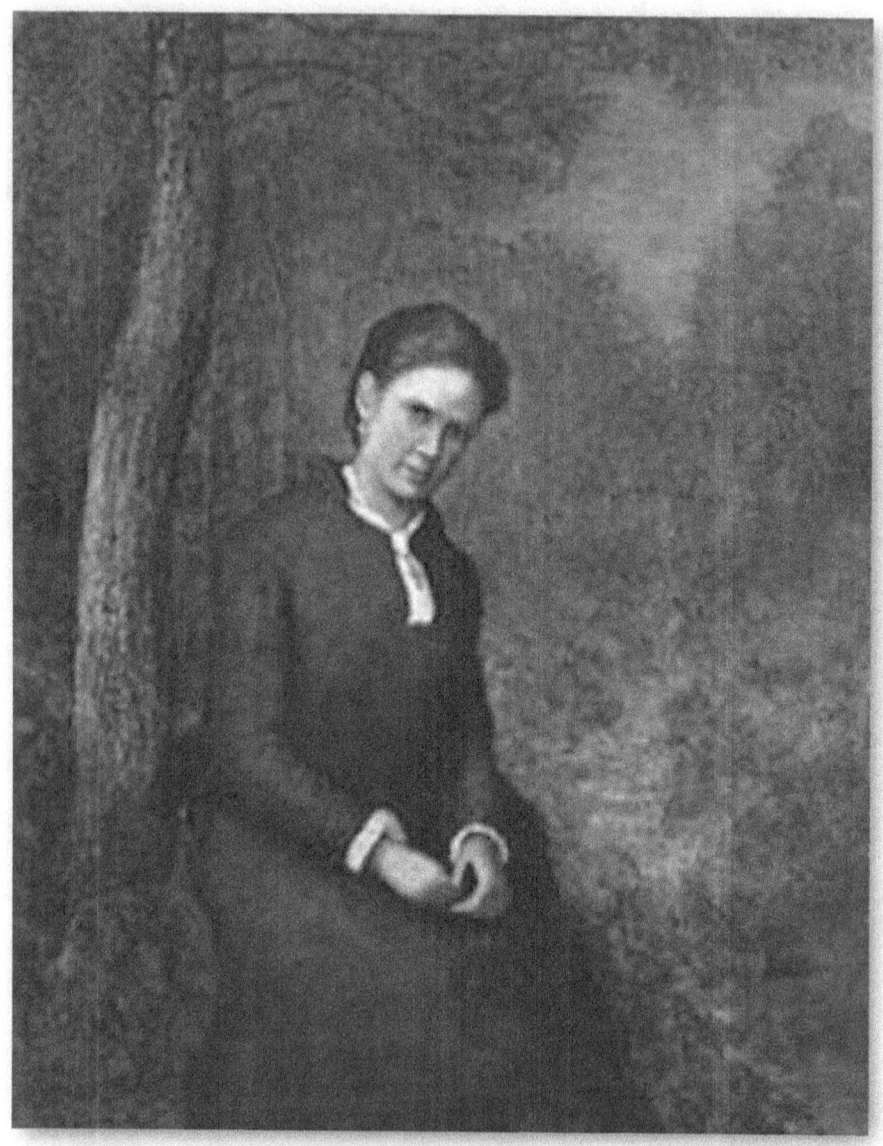

Figure 3. Cora Bailey (later Mrs. Ralph Blakelock), 1875. Oil on canvas, 20 1/4 × 16 1/4 in. (51.4 × 41.3 cm). Fine Arts Museums of San Francisco, California. Memorial gift from Dr. T. Edward and Tullah Hanley.

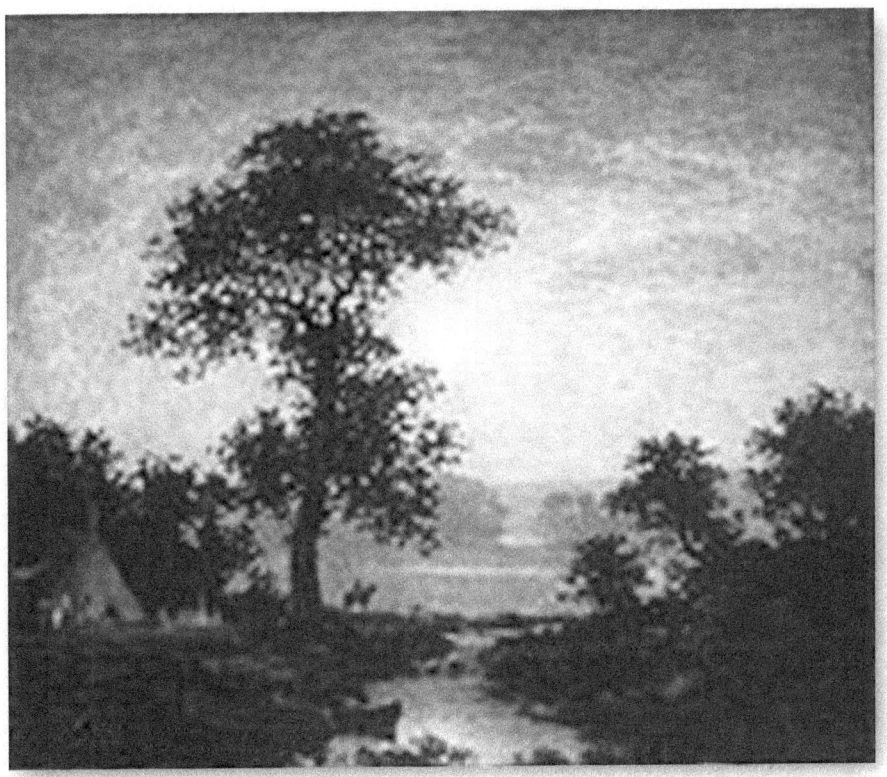

Figure 4. Ralph Albert Blakelock, *Moonlight*, ca 1885–89. Oil on canvas, 27 1/16 × 32 in. (68.7 × 81.3 cm). Brooklyn Museum, New York. Dick S. Ramsay Fund.

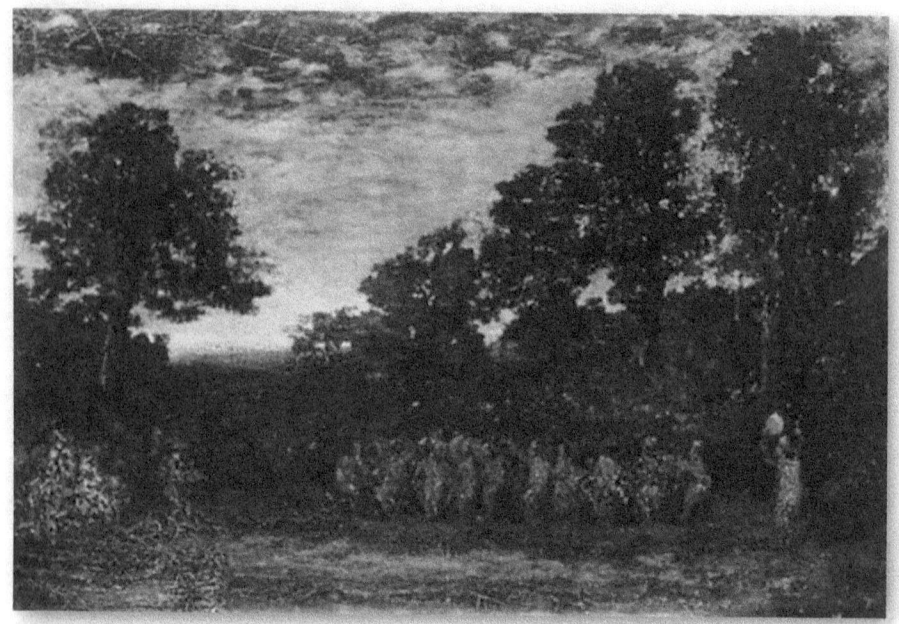

Figure 5. Ralph Albert Blakelock, *The Pipe Dance*, ca. 1880–1900. Oil on canvas, 48 1/2 × 72 in. (123.2 × 182.9 cm). Metropolitan Museum of Art, New York. Gift of George A. Hearn, 1909. Accession no. 09.25.01.

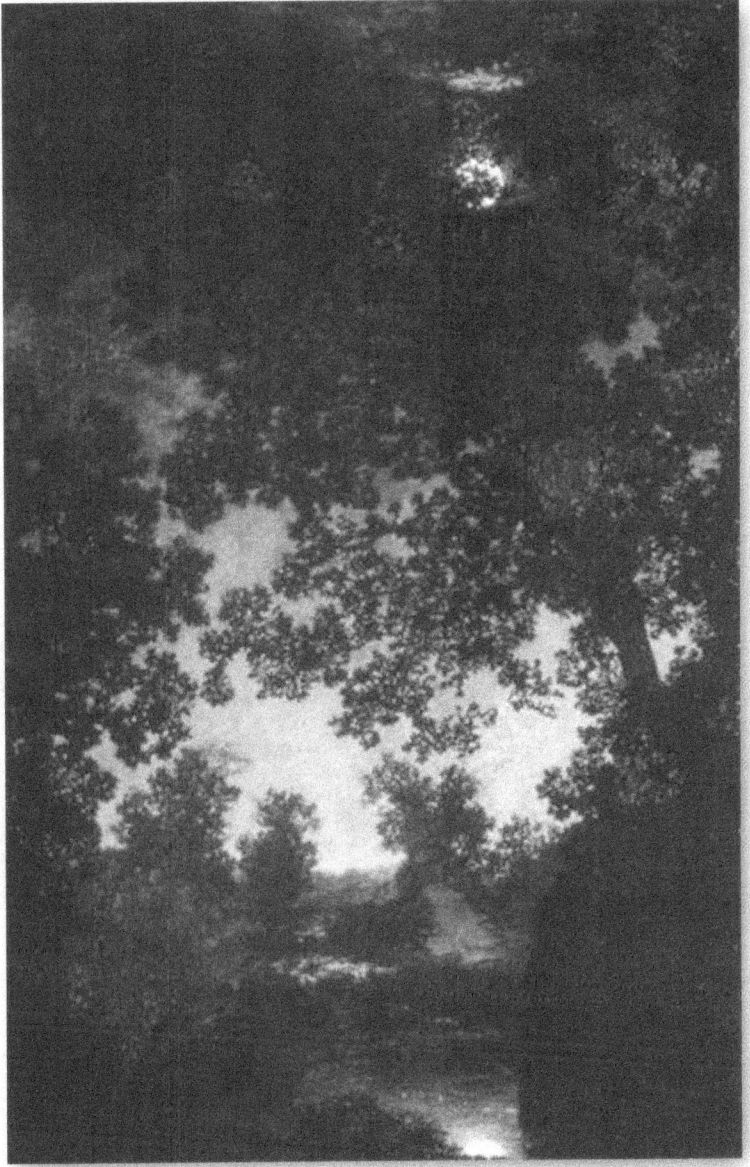

Figure 6, Ralph Albert Blakelock, *Brook by Moonlight*, pre-1891. Oil on canvas, 72 1/8 × 48 1/16 in. (183.2 × 122.1 cm). Toledo Museum of Art, Ohio. Gift of Mr. and Mrs. Edward Drummond Libbey.

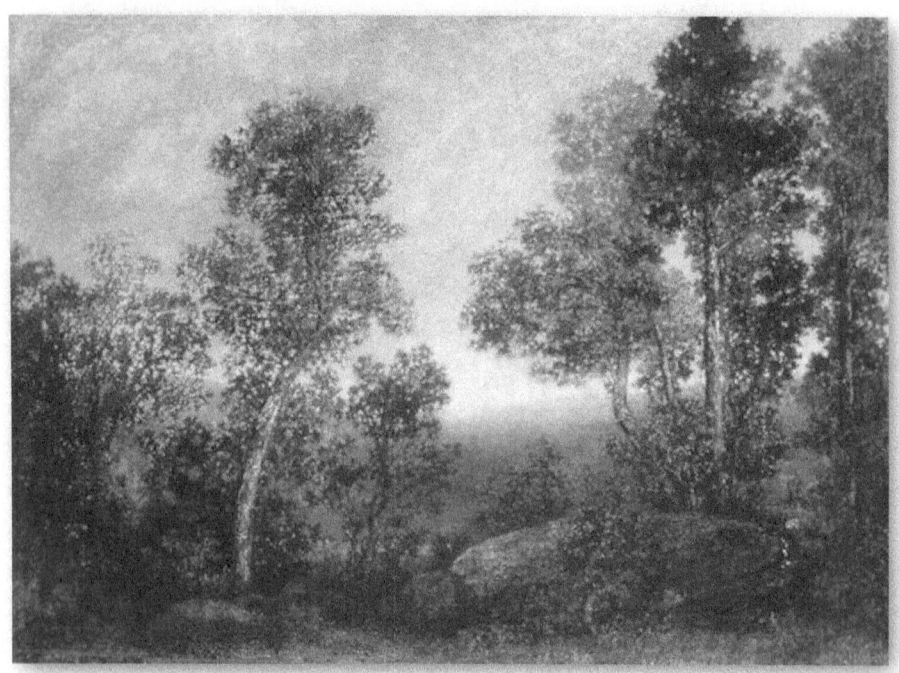

Figure 7. Ralph Albert Blakelock, *Landscape*, 1885–95. Oil on canvas, 27 × 37 3/8 in. (68.6 × 94.9 cm). Metropolitan Museum of Art, New York. Gift of the nieces of Harmon W. Hendricks. Accession no. 29.35.

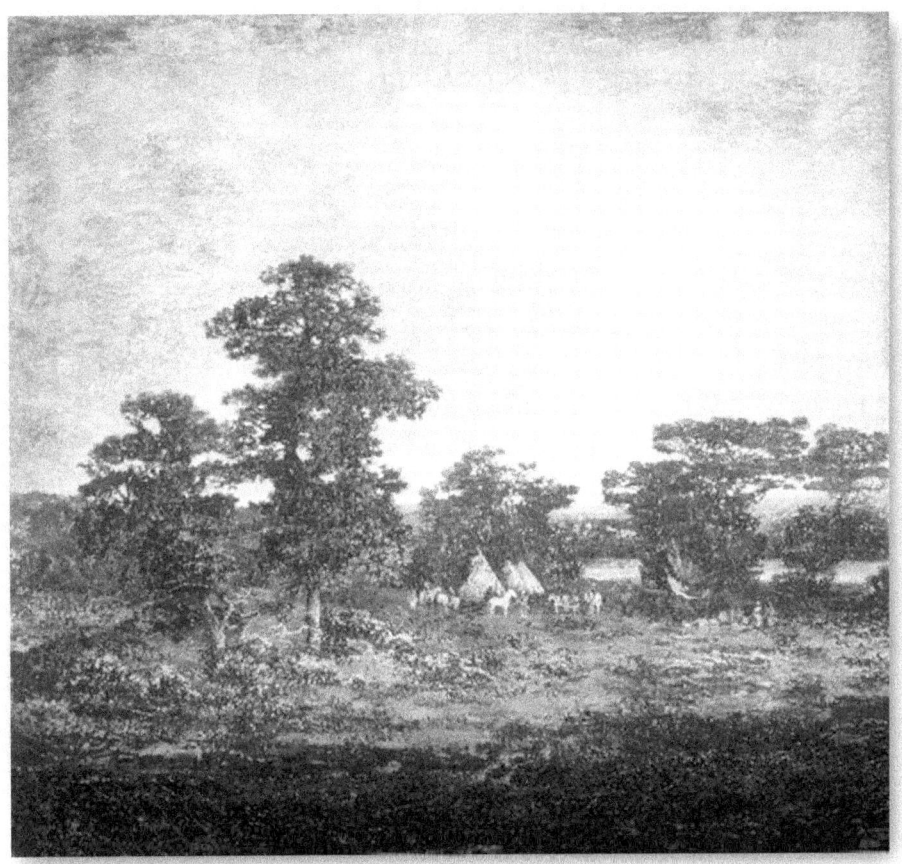

Figure 8. Ralph Albert Blakelock, *An Indian Encampment*, ca. 1880–90. Oil on canvas, 37 5/8 × 40 5/8 in. (95.6 × 103.2 cm). Metropolitan Museum of Art, New York. Gift of George A. Hearn. Accession no. 06.1269.

HOMER DODGE MARTIN: IMPAIRED
EYESIGHT AND ARTISTIC VISION

Homer Dodge Martin (fig. 1) was born on October 28, 1836, and died at the age of 61, on February 12, 1887, his life cut short by a throat cancer that spread throughout his body. Always a landscape painter, he carried the tradition of the Hudson River School through romanticism, Barbizon, tonalism, and finally expressionism. His colleagues George Inness and Alexander Helwig Wyant received the recognition that he also deserved. Martin never even had the brief flurry of success that Ralph Albert Blakelock, who was confined to a mental institution at the time. All these great landscape painters, the last of their kind, suffered from some form of debilitation. Inness had epilepsy, while Blakelock spent the last twenty years of his life confined to a mental institution. Wyant had stroke damage on his right side and had to learn to paint with his left hand, while Martin had vision problems that did not allow him to paint straight or perpendicular lines and eventually led to blindness. With the optic nerve in one eye dead and the other clouded by cataracts, in the last year of his life, Martin told his wife: "I have learned to paint at last. If I were quite blind now and knew just where the colors were on my palette, I could express myself."[40] Homer Dodge Martin deserves the recognition that was denied him in his lifetime.

---

40   Elizabeth Gilbert Martin, *Homer Martin: A Reminiscence, October 28, 1836–February 12, 1897* (New York: William Macbeth, 1904), 49.

THE ARTIST'S LIFE

Martin was the fourth and youngest child of Homer Martin and Sarah Dodge. He was born on October 28, 1836, the same year as Alexander Helwig Wyant, in a house on Park Street, in Albany, New York. His mother said that he began drawing at the age of twenty months: she would give him a blank paper and pencil to quiet him down. Although he liked to read, he was a very poor student, spending his time looking through the windows of the classroom. Upon leaving school, he worked in his father's carpenter shop, then as a clerk there, and finally in an architect's office, doing very poorly in all these positions. He attempted to enlist in the army at the start of the Civil War but was rejected because of "the defects" in his vision. At the age of sixteen, a local Albany sculptor encouraged Martin's father to give him his own studio for painting. With little or no training, he began to paint and to sell his artwork.

Martin married on June 25, 1861,[41] and in 1863 went to New York and at first shared a studio with James Smillie, another artist. In 1865 he secured his own small studio in the Tenth Street Studio Building, which he maintained until sailing to England, for a second time, in 1881. Martin had exhibited at the National Academy of Design as early as 1857. In 1868 he was elected an associate of the Academy and in 1874 was made a full academician. In the early 1860s he went to the White Mountains, and from 1864 to 1869 he went to the Adirondacks every summer. In 1871 he went to Duluth, Minnesota, at the invitation of the financier Jay Cooke, and in 1872 he went to the Smoky Mountains in North Carolina. In 1877 he was invited as a founding member of the Society of American Artists.[42]

Martin's landscapes were often commissioned, and it was rare that a painting remained long on the easel before being sold. According to his wife, they had an income averaging between $2,000 (roughly $29,500 in 2014 dollars) and $3,000 ($44,300) annually, and sometimes even higher. His wife supplemented his income by writing book reviews while raising their family. Martin went to France, Holland, and England in 1876, where he visited the Barbizon

---

41   Ibid., 3–12.

42   John Charles Van Dyke, *American Painting and Its Tradition* (New York: Charles Scribner's Sons, 1919), 72–76.

painters and established a friendship with James McNeill Whistler. In 1881, he was sent to England by *The Century Magazine* to prepare some illustrations of George Eliot's country, an assignment he considered hackwork but he was pleased to be able to have his wife join him.[43] From England, Martin went to the Continent but mainly traveled through northern France. He did little painting there, mainly just absorbing all the ideas and concepts he was seeing. They had little money and would wait for sales of his paintings to pay their bills. His wife referred to this period as "a time of absorption rather than production," a "seed time."[44] When he returned, he painted several pictures similar to *Normandy Coast* (fig. 6) and *Criquebeof Church, Normandy* (fig. 8)

Martin arrived back in New York on December 12, 1886, using a room in his apartment on 63rd Street before finding a studio on 55th Street. In 1890 he took a studio in a house belonging to the Paulist Fathers, adjacent to their convent on 59th Street. In the summer of 1892, he and his wife sailed to England and spent most of their time in the coastal town of Bournemouth. Martin's eyesight continued to deteriorate and in June 1893, he and his wife moved to St. Paul Minnesota to be with their oldest son. In 1894, he returned for one last time to New York to be present at a Century Club reunion where he received some recognition for his work.[45]

During the early 1890s the members of the Century Association gathered a purse of $80 ($2,110) to $100 ($2,640) to buy Martin's work at the Artists' Fund Exhibitions, "knowing full well no one else would bid on them and wishing in a friendly way to save him the mortification of having his pictures withdrawn."[46] In lieu of a membership fee, he gave the Century Association *Ausable Valley and Mount Mercey* (figs. 5 and 5A), which is still at the headquarters.[47] His use of bright colors alienated him from the usual

---

43 Martin, *Homer Martin: A Reminiscence*, 13–22.

44 Ibid., 36, 39.

45 Ibid., 44–51.

46 "New York Art," *Brush and Pencil* 5, no. 6 (1900): 270–73, http://www.jstor.org/stable/25505523.

47 The Association's curator, Jonathan Harding, informed me that it was common practice to accept paintings from artists in lieu of the membership fee, which was difficult for them to afford.

market for Hudson River School paintings. In 1892 the "100 members" of the Century Association had purchased *Honfleur Light* (fig. 3), which is also still at the building, for $1,100 ($29,000) to permit Martin one final trip to France. It is why as a sick man he traveled from St. Paul for the reunion.

Although almost blind, he continued to paint and produced powerful landscapes that combined his prior recollections with his inner visions. A professor of ophthalmology writing in 2008 believed that Martin suffered from cataracts and that his works reveal changes in details and colors as he aged.[48] In October 1896 he was diagnosed with throat cancer, which spread to his brain and from which he died on February 12, 1897. Before dying, his wife told him that she intended to enter a convent, to which he replied: "Well it is a beautiful life."[49]

Only after his death did Martin's popularity increase and his pictures come into wider esteem. Many of his paintings were forged and faked to meet the newfound demand that had passed him by in his lifetime.[50] Although a member of the three chief New York exhibiting societies, he had never received any prize or honor for his paintings.[51]

THE ARTIST

The introduction to his wife's biography of Martin describes him as "so intensely masculine, so preeminently a man's man, that he must necessarily have escaped through comprehension by any woman."[52] He was also described by an English acquaintance as being dressed in "shabby black clothes . . . fit only for the dust heap . . . and a marked deficiency in clean linen" with his face being "distressingly disfigured by drink—all red and pimpled" who "did

48   James G. Ravin, "The Visual Difficulties of Selected Artists and Limitations of Ophthalmological Care During the 19th and Early 20th Centuries," *Transactions of the American Opthalmological Society* 106 (2008): 402–25.

49   Martin, *Homer Martin: A Reminiscence*, 55–58.

50   Van Dyke, *American Painting and Its Tradition*, 87.

51   Frank Jewett Mather, *Homer Martin, Poet in Landscape* (New York: Frederic Fairchild Sherman, 1912), 9.

52   Martin, *Homer Martin: A Reminiscence*, vii.

not talk much and listened courteously." Whistler once introduced him thus: "Gentlemen, this is Homer Martin, He doesn't look as if he were, but he is." The artist George Boughton preferred not having him in his studio because "so deterrent was his effect upon conventionally minded British patrons."[53] The American artist Elihu Vedder described him as "fond of or loving painting, stories, beer or his friends." Vedder goes on to say that when Martin was asked whether he drank too much beer, the reply was "I don't think there is too much beer."[54]

Martin was always friendly and companionable and had something of a genius for making friends. Throughout his life he maintained social relations with the wise and witty, moving in intellectual and creative circles. He always had droll and clever comments. This contrasted greatly with his paintings, all landscapes, which were serious and often melancholy. There were never any people in his paintings and they were never intended to be narrative or informative. They simply reflected what he saw in nature.[55]

Martin was a lifelong agnostic, but his wife became deeply religious and converted to Catholicism in 1870.[56] The Paulist Fathers gave him a studio near their convent when he needed one. His wife did enter a convent after his death, and the writing of the biography was started in while she was there.[57] Based on his wife's biography, it also appears that he was a family man; his wife was most certainly devoted to him. Toward the end of his life, he and his wife went to live with their eldest son to be near their grandchildren and to have someone to look after them.

Throughout his life, Martin was unappreciated and had to struggle. Through his paintings, he sought self-control, not emotional release. He was temperamentally a classicist who sought not to replicate actual classical or Renaissance precedent but to apply the classical approach to landscape.

---

53 Mather, *Homer Martin, Poet in Landscape*, 7.

54 Patricia C. F. Mandel, "The Stories behind Three Important Late Homer D. Martin Paintings," *Archives of American Art Journal* 13, no. 3 (1973): 2–8, http://www.jstor.org/stable/1557094.

55 Van Dyke, *American Painting and Its Tradition*, 67–72.

56 Mather, *Homer Martin, Poet in Landscape*, 24.

57 Mandel, "The Stories behind Three Important Homer D. Martin Paintings," 4.

Lacking even minimal formal training, Martin had to develop his own approach. This caused much frustration in his early career and produced periods of sterility in later life. His problematic eyesight also caused him to rely on his inner vision in conjunction with the images he had seen and wished to record. He did not paint vague images to incite the viewer's own emotions but rather forced the viewer to see his own vision.[58] A good example would be *Effect of Trees* (fig. 7).

Martin never had any positive theory of art that he tried to work out in his paintings. He painted instinctively toward a given goal. He understood the dramatic effect of being able to emphasize certain features of a landscape by suppressing others.[59] He did things that were not done by other American painters. In his paintings, Martin left elements out or merely indicated them, while slurring local color for general tone. By the early 1870s he began using colors that were never or rarely seen in nature, thus removing him from the tradition of Kensett, Church, and Durand, who were more familiar to the collecting public. He often displayed traditionally blue skies as vibrant green. There was no cleverness in his pictures—just breathless, painstaking reverence.[60] *In the Adirondacks* (fig. 4) is fairly typical of his work.

As a struggling young artist, Martin was greatly influenced by the Hudson River School and was by Kensett, who was beginning to achieve fame, in particular. Many believe that it was Martin who transmitted Kensett's landscape style to the younger generation of American artists.[61] Martin maintained the draftsmanship of Kensett, but he greatly broadened his dark, dull palette by using brighter colors, particularly reds. Many feel that Martin, in his middle period, surpassed Kensett because "the contrast between the execution and the conception is the same."[62] Martin's composition is less commonplace than

---

58 James Thomas Flexner, *That Wilder Image: The Painting of America's Native School from Thomas Cole to Winslow Homer* (Boston: Little, Brown, 1962), 327.

59 Van Dyke, *American Painting and Its Tradition*, 80.

60 Mather, *Homer Martin, Poet in Landscape*, 10.

61 F. J. M. Jr., "An Enigmatic American Landscape," *Record of the Museum of Historic Art* 4, no. 1 (1945): 4, http://www.jstor.org/stable/3774145.

62 Samuel Isham, *The History of American Painting* (New York: MacMillan, 1936), 240.

Kensett's, with better line and mass and more true to the actual landscape: "The edges of the mountains against the sky and the shores of the lake are sharp and fine . . . but drawn with infinite delicacy; while the masses of the forests and hills are kept simple and simple in spite of the multiplicity of detail."[63]

Martin received good reviews, but his paintings sold slowly. A review of one of his exhibitions in 1873 focused on his *A White Mountain Brook* and *Lake Mohonk*, describing him as "an industrious, painstaking artist, well known in New York, who devotes himself to landscape paintings entirely. His pictures have a characteristic somber quietness about them". His paintings are described in poetic terms as blending "the gloomy, the grand, the picturesque in a scene which is full of sublimity."[64]

In reviewing an exhibition of American artists held in November 1880, the *Art Journal* goes to great lengths to describe Martin's landscapes as having "a singularly artistic quality," wagering that the reader was "likely to be attracted to them. No matter how brilliant is the company in which, for the moment, they may be." The review then goes on to bemoan the fact that "his works have not sold commensurately with their deserts." The review lays the blame on his paintings: "being native productions, they are not so fashionable as foreign ones. Although Martin has a 'fondness for colour' . . . and . . . 'an accomplished and laborious draftsman', he must await America setting its own fashions rather than following the 'modern Fontainebleau school' . . . and such artists as Corot, Rousseau, Daubigny, Dupres and Diaz despite the fact that he uses color as well as they do."[65]

Martin's style did evolve over time, starting with his arrival in New York in 1862, where he became familiar with Kensett's work. Like Kensett's, his pictures were composed of a few large forms, with each form containing within itself much small detail. He also gave a considerable amount

---

63 Ibid., 262.

64 Chandos Fulton, "A White Mountain Brook", *The Aldine* 6, no. 11 (1873): 218–19. http:// www.jstor.org/stable/20636651.

65 "American Painters: Homer D. Martin," *Art Journal (1875–1880)*, n.s., 6 (1880): 321–23, http://www.jstor.org/stable/20569595.

attention to the edges where shapes meet or are silhouetted against the sky. Many regarded his paintings of the 1870s as glorified versions of Kensett's work, but with the addition "of nerve, substance and higher seriousness."[66] In the early 1870s, Martin developed a style similar to Corot's, in using color to suggest the small details rather than drawing them out. Unfortunately, he then began to use much brighter pigments that did not fit with the landscapes, thereby removing himself from the public's taste for Hudson River School paintings. His painting practice began to dwindle, and he did not start painting in earnest again until his return in 1886 from his four-year visit to France.

He absorbed some of the concepts of the French impressionists, but his contemplative painting was incompatible with their instantaneous reaction to the moment. He did absorb the space, hue, and atmosphere so beloved by the impressionists.[67] He never showed the sensibilities of impressionism that became popular in American painters of the next generation, but he did incorporate some of their techniques into his paintings.

The 1880s was a cruel period of time for almost all American artists. The Hudson River School was collapsing and rapidly losing favor, while the two main exhibiting locations in New York, the Academy and the Society, were feuding. The arrival in New York of international dealers, primarily from France and England, further shifted the emphasis of the collecting public away from American painters.[68]

Martin continued to paint landscapes his entire life. Writing a little later, Birge Harrison noted a shift by many painters away from still-life painting to landscapes. He believed that the chief cause was "the fact that our lives are not, humanly speaking, so beautiful as they once were. Our clothing is no longer picturesque. The advent of farm machinery has destroyed much of the pastoral and bucolic beauty of country life."[69]

---

66 Mather, *Homer Martin, Poet in Landscape*, 37–38.

67 Flexner, *That Wilder Image*, 330–32.

68 Mather, *Homer Martin, Poet in Landscape*, 54.

69 Birge Harrison, "The Future of American Art," *North American Review* 189, no. 638 (1909): 25–34, http://www.jstor.org/stable/25106273.

By 1900 there had been a strong revival in American art: "The best of the men were represented in this direction, the list being headed by the veterans— all dead alas!—George Inness, Homer Martin, and Alexander H. Wyant. They are named in order of their strength."[70] It should be noted that both Inness and Wyant had substantially more successful careers than Martin's.

In 1892 the "100 members" of the Century Association[71] had purchased *Honfleur Light* (see figs. 3 and 3A) for $1,100 ($29,000) to permit Martin one final trip back to France. *Harp of the Winds* (fig. 2), his most famous painting, was probably purchased for $1,500 ($39,600).[72] In 1893, William T. Evans purchased *An Old Church in Normandy* directly from Martin for $500 ($13,400). The prices of his almost unsalable pictures had also dramatically risen with *Normandy Trees*, selling in 1899 for $2,850 ($81,600), and *Westchester Hills*, for $4,750 ($136,000).[73]

At the sale of the Clarke collection in 1899, an unidentified 20 × 32" painting went for $1,500 ($43,000), and *Adirondack Scenery* sold for $5,000 ($145,000).[74] Clarke had paid $400 ($11,400) for this picture three years prior. A smaller picture, *Wild Cherry Trees*, was also sold for $175 ($5,070), for which Clarke had paid approximately $30 ($859). *Adirondack Scenery* had been purchased at the 1899 sale by Samuel Untermyer and was sold in 1940 for $2,000 ($32,200) to William Macbeth, who sold it to Arthur D. Whiteside, and was sold in 1961 for $300 ($2,340). Patricia C. F. Mandel tracked down the painting in 1969, which was in private hands and insured for $10,000 ($63,500).

In 1890 Clarke had purchased *Source of the Hudson*, then known as *Headwaters of the Hudson*, at auction for $270 ($7,130), which was sold at his 1899 sale for $1500 ($39,600). In 1901 at the Milliken sale, *Westchester Hills*

---

70 "Appreciation in Value of American Paintings," 271.

71 I only recently became aware that the Century Association was still in existence and was given a tour of their collection by the curator, Dr. Jonathan Harding. Seeing the Hudson River paintings in their proper setting further highlights their appeal and beauty.

72 Mandel, "The Stories behind Three Important Late Homer D. Martin Paintings," 8.

73 Ibid., 272.

74 Linda Skalet, "Thomas B. Clarke, American Collector," *Archives of American Art Journal* 5, no. 3 (1975): 52–83, http://www.jstor.org/stable/1557068.

was sold for $5,300 ($141,000).[75] Dr. Alexander C. Humphreys had written to Martin's widow that he had been offered this painting several times for $100 ($2,900) when it was "kicking around among dealers." In 1899, it had been sold by the Macbeth Gallery to William T. Evans for $1,000 ($29,000). In 1912, Robert W. Vonnoh wrote that the painting would bring $30,000 ($743,000).[76]

Writing about the Comparative Exhibition of 1905 held at the Fine Arts Building in New York, Samuel Swift describes Martin's paintings as American art at its best, comparing the "ripe perfection" to that of Delacroix and Corot and concluding, "Here was something thoroughly American, wholly precious, something worthy of our respect and admiration."[77] It was just unfortunate that Martin had been long since dead.

This belated recognition continued through the 1920s. In a talk given at the Cleveland Museum in 1924, Royal Cortissoz bemoaned the massive collection of Italian art and thanked the trustees for also purchasing American art. He acknowledged the work of Stuart and Copley but stated firmly that "we do not become fully Americanized until the rise of Homer Martin, Inness, John LaFarge, Whistler, Winslow Homer and Wyant . . . who made our golden age." He went on to say that Martin "paints nature as if seen through a temperament" so that each of his works is "unmistakably a Martin." He concluded, "Our pioneers such as Homer and Martin influenced a great many of the men who came after them."[78]

A POSTHUMOUS HISTORY OF THE ARTIST'S POPULARITY AND ART PRICES

This study starts in 1946, when a new generation of collectors, critics, and scholars came on the scene with the aftermath of World War II. Pricing from

---

75 "Appreciation in Values of American Paintings," 14–15.

76 Mandel, "The Stories behind Three Important Late Homer D. Martin Paintings," 3–6.

77 Samuel Swift, "Americanism in Art," *Brush and Pencil* 15, no. 1 (1905): 57, http://www.jstor/stable/25503769.

78 Royal Cortissoz, "Informal Talk by Royal Cortissoz," *Bulletin of the Cleveland Museum of Art* 11, no. 4 (1924): 84–86, http://www.jstor.org/stable/2513676.

1946 to 1984 is based on *World Collectors Annuary*[79] (almost all auctions cited being from Parke-Bernet) and from 1986 to 2014 on Artnet.[80] For ease of comparison, current price equivalents have been placed in parentheses.[81] When more than five paintings were sold at auction in any year, the highest price is listed, followed by the range of high and low prices for the remainder. There are sometimes large time gaps, but it is not clear whether this is due to no auction sales having occurred or simple clerical omissions.[82]

1946

Criquebeouf Church, Normandy, 23 × 36" $250 ($2,980)
The Old Mill, 30 × 56", described by Mrs. Martin in her biography $375 ($4,470)

1947

On the Coast, 15 1/2 × 24" from Clarke Collection $135 ($1,410)

1951

Landscape, 30 × 60" from Louis Marshall, New York $150 ($1,350)

1957

Criquebeouf Church, Normandy (see Fig. 8), 66 × 96 ½" from Samuel Untermyer $1000 ($8,280)

---

79 A. M. E. Van Eijk Van Voorthusijsen, ed., *World Collectors Annuary* (Delft, Netherlands: Brouwer, n.d.).

80 Artnet Price Database, accessed January 12, 2015, http://www.artnet.com/PDA/FAADsearch/FAADResults3.aspx?page=1&ArtType=F.

81 Measuring Worth, accessed January 12, 2015, http://www.measuringworth.com/uscompare.

82

1965

Near North Creek, 15 × 20" from BF Jones, Kleemann Galleries $900 ($6,640)
The Giant Dead River Pond, Adirondacks, 18 × 30" from Kleemann Galleries $1200 ($

1968

Seaview, 7 1/2 × 11" $700 ($4,690)
Lake George, 7 × 9 ¾ $375 ($2,510)

1970

The Adirondacks, 15 × 24" $4,000 ($24,000)
Lake George, 14 × 24" $2,000 ($12,000)

1973

Lake Ontario, 14 × 22" from O'Donnell Iselin $3,900 ($20,400)
Landscape, 15 1/2 × 27 ¾" $3,750 ($19,700)

1975

Rocks, 43.2 × 58.3 cm. $1,400 ($6,060)

1976

Wooded Landscape, 46 × 76.5 cm. $1,700 ($6,960)

1977

Westchester Hills, 33 1/2 × 60 ¼" Exh. Whitney Museum 1940 $7,000 ($26,900)

1978

Lowtide Honfleur, 18 1/2 × 32 ½" $2,800 ($10,000)

1987

The Giant Dead River Pond, 18.4 × 30.3" Christie's New York $4,950 ($10,200)

1989

Sketch of the Adirondack's, 8.6 × 10.5" Christie's East $1,980 ($3,720)

1990

In the Adirondacks (see Fig. 4), 18 × 28", Sotheby's Arcade $14,300 ($25,500)
Mount Hood – Oregon, 11 × 17.9" Phillips London $1,312 ($2,340)
Forest, 11.5 × 17" Freeman's $325 ($579)

1991

Fall Landscape, 11.3 × 17.5" DuMouchelles $2,500 ($4,280)
Canadian Landscape, 11 × 16.5" Wolf's $1,200 ($2,050)
Road to the Village Waterfront, Low Tide, 12 × 16", Christie's New York $1,980 ($3,390)
Moon at Sunset, 18 × 30" Sharon Boccelli $2,500 ($4,280)

1992

East Hampton, 12 × 20" Christie's New York $6,050 ($10,000)
Lake George, 13 × 24", Sotheby's New York $22,000 ($36,500)

1993

Country Landscape with a Valley in the Distance, 14 × 20" Wechler's $3,740 ($6,030)

Woodland Scene, 12 × 10" Eldred's $1,540 ($2,480)
Richmond on Thames, 6.6 × 11.8" Louisiana Auction $1,750 ($2,820)

1994

Deer in Mountain Landscape, 14 × 22" Barridoff $2,860 ($4,500)
Rushing River, 19 × 14" Mystic Fine Arts $3,300 ($5,190)
The Moon at Sunset, 17.8 × 30" Skinner $1,840 ($2,890)

1995

By the River, 14 × 22" Mystic Fine Art $2,860 $4,370
A Clearing through the Trees, 4.5 × 10" C.G. Sloan $750 ($1,150)
The Moon at Sunset, 18 × 30" Mystic Fine Art $2,420 ($3,700)

1996

Fire Island, 8 × 14.1" Sotheby's Arcade $7,475 ($11,100)
Autumn Twilight, 10 × 16" Young Fine Arts $1,200 ($1,780)
Autumn Boating in the Adirondacks, 11 × 21" Sotheby's New York $4,312 ($6,400)
Landscape, 5.5 × 9.5" Grogan $2,185 ($3,240)
Bringing in the Hay, 11.2 × 16.3" Weschler's $3,335 ($4,950)

1997

Inlet, 9 × 14" Mystic Fine Arts $1,064 ($1,540)
Sunset, 8.5 × 12.6" Christie's East $5,980 ($8,680)
View of Lake George from the North End of Long Island, 13 × 23" Doyle New York $17,250 ($25,000)
Boy Fishing, 19.5 × 29.5 Leslie Hindman $3,000 ($4,350)
Evening Landscape, 17 × 27" Eldred's $440 ($639)

1998

Cabin in a Landscape at Sunset, 8 × 12" Christie's East $1,840 ($2,630)
Cascading Falls, 30 × 20" Dunning's $2,300 ($3,290)
The Adirondacks, 8.5 × 10.5" Sotheby's Arcade $6,900 ($9,860)
Adirondack Landscape, 18 × 32" Christie's East $5,175 ($7,400)
The River at Dusk, 24.3 × 36" Christie's East $8,625 ($12,300)

1999

River Landscape, 18 × 30" Shannon's $2,464 ($3,450)
Toward the Adirondacks, 32 × 26" Christie's East $5,750 ($8,040)
The Waterfall, 26 × 14" Christie's New York $40,250 ($56,300)
Autumn Landscape with Pumpkin Patch, 12.8 × 20.5" Butterfields $13,800 ($19,300)

2000

Autumn Mountain Landscape, 12 × 20" Neal Auction $3,300 ($4,460)
Autumn Sunset on the Lake, 10 × 15.5" Skinner $1,495 ($2,020)
Morning Mist, Lake George, 12 × 20" Shannon's $23,000 ($31,100)
Misty Morning on the Hudson River, 10 × 20" Phillips New York $5,175 ($7,000)

2001

Sunset on Lake George, 12 × 18" Sotheby's New York $26,625 ($35,000)
Southern Landscape with Live Oak and Palm 18 × 30.5" Shannon's $18,400 ($24,200)
Silver Lake, 24.5 × 40.2" Phillips dePury & Luxembourgh $23,000 ($30,300)
Cows and Sheep Grazing on an Autumn River Landscape, 20 × 36" Christie's East $7,050 ($9,270)
Cascading Falls, 30 × 20" Shannon's $5,750 ($7,560)

2002

A Waterfall in a Wooded Landscape, 36 × 22 Butterfield's $9,400 ($12,200)
Early Spring, 7.2 × 9.8" Freeman's $1,763 ($2,280)

2003

Silence of the Brooks, 7 × 11.2" Shannon's $8,225 ($10,400)
Mountain Landscape in Autumn, 16 × 14" Shannon's $14,100 ($17,900)
A View of the Lake, 14 × 24" Shannon's $21,150 ($26,800)

2004

Sunset, 8.5 × 12.5" Christie's New York $8,963 ($11,100)

2005

Toward the Adirondacks, 32 × 26" Christie's New York $10,200 ($12,200)
Twilight by the River, 22 × 28" Heritage Auctions $2,390 ($2,850)
Twilight Stream, 22 × 36.2" Shannon's $9,560 ($11,400)

2006

Autumn in the Adirondacks, 22 × 25.7" Christie's New York $10,200 ($11,800)

2007

Low Tide, Villerville, 12.5 × 20.7" Sotheby's New York $20,000 (22,500)
Nine (9) other paintings also sold that year at auction ranging in price from $1,793 ($2,010) to $19,200 ($21,600).

2008

The White Mountains, 30 × 50" Christie's New York $20,000 ($21,600)
Overlooking the Valley, 18 × 34" Barridorf Galleries $36,000 (($39,000)

2009

Rocky Stream, 6.5 × 9" Shannon's $7,800 ($8,470)
South Side of Long Island, 15.5 × 24.5" Barridorf Galleries $$14,400 ($15,600)

2010

Mountain Sunset, 14 × 12" Trinity International $41,000 ($43,800)
View, 12 × 18", DuMouchelles $8,500 ($9,080)

2011

Dusk in the Lake, 12.2 × 20.2" Leslie Hindman $21,960 ($22,700)
Seven (7) other paintings were sold that year at auction ranging in price from $1,600 ($1,660) to $12,500 ($12,900).

2012

View over the Valley, 25 × 35" Leslie Hindman $3,172

2013

The River at Dusk, 24 × 36" Dallas Auction Gallery $4,750

2014

Waterfall, 21 × 16" Barridorf Galleries $7,440
Sun Breaking over a Lake with Deer Grazing, 23.9 × 40.1" Brunk Auctions $3,600

CONCLUSION

Homer Dodge Martin was different from many of the artists of his time, and that hindered him in obtaining the recognition he deserved. He passed through life as a hard-working, thoughtful, and creative artist who could not appeal to the collecting public. The posthumous prices of his paintings seem to reflect the same. Even many years after his death, the prices and his recognition seem to fluctuate randomly. The upswing in prices and interest in nineteenth-century American art, which occurred from the late 1970s through 2000, may have had the most impact upon Martin's prices and the increased sales at auction of his paintings.

Figures

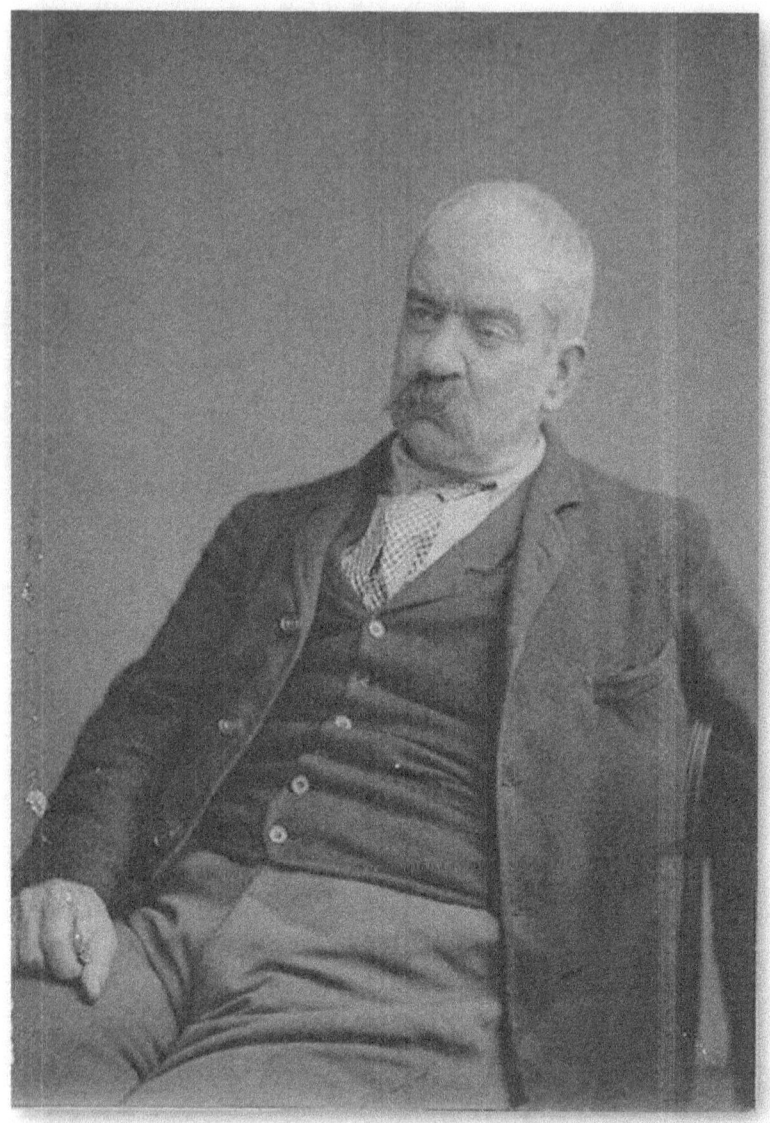

Figure 1. Homer Dodge Martin, Enfield, England, 1892. Black-and-white photographic print, 16 × 11 cm (photographer unknown). Smithsonian Institution, Washington, DC.

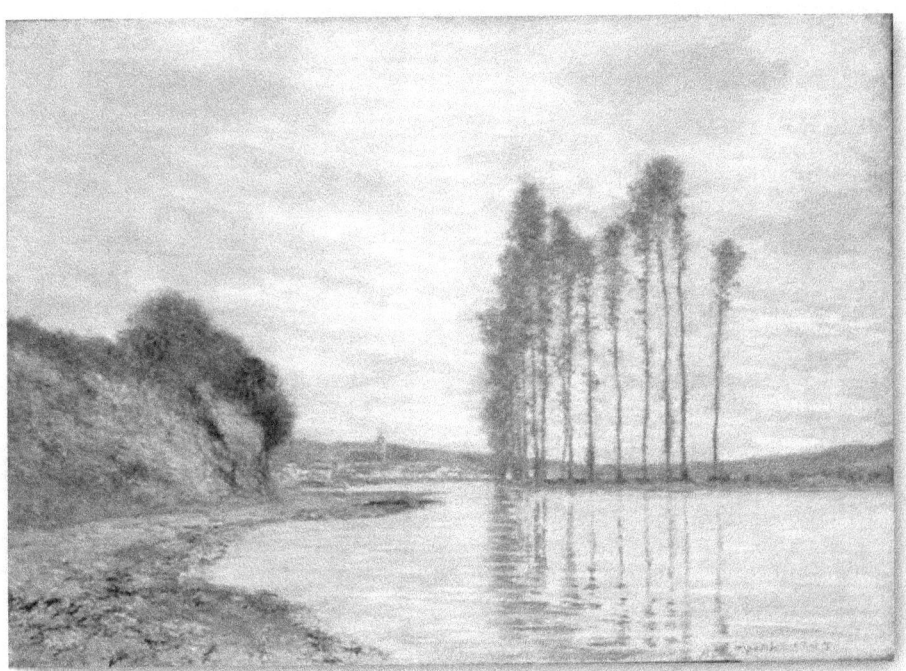

Figure 2. Homer Dodge Martin, *View on the Seine: Harp of the Winds*, 1893 95. Oil on canvas, 28 3/4 × 40 3/4 in. (73 × 103.5 cm). Metropolitan Museum of Art, New York.

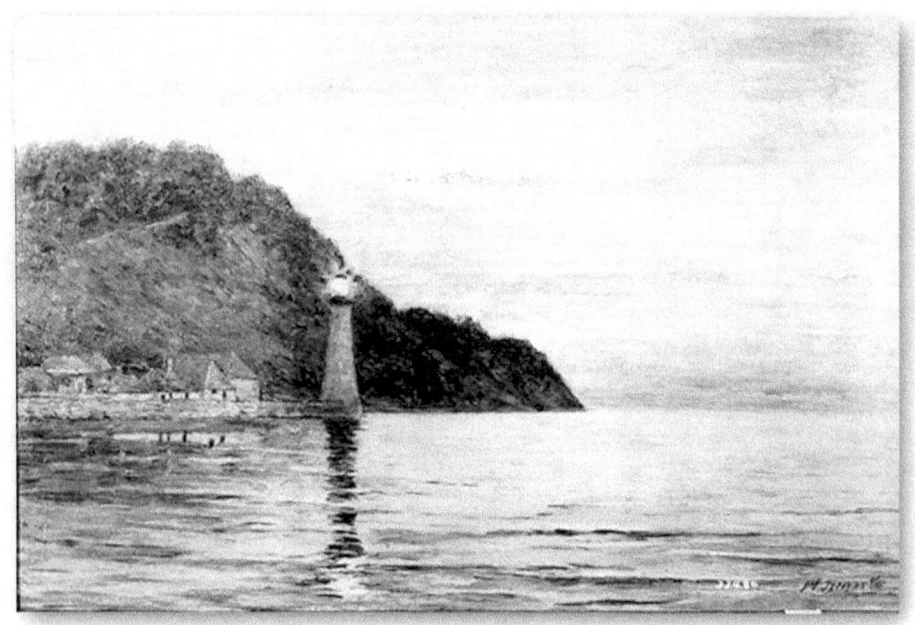

Figure 3. Homer Dodge Martin, *Honfleur Light*, 1890–92. Oil on canvas, 23 × 36 (sight) in. Century Association, New York.

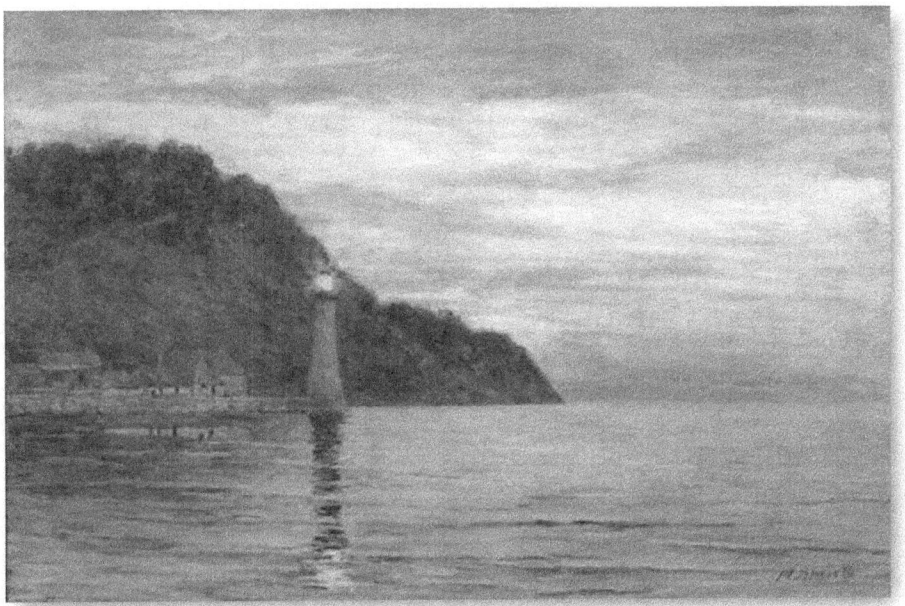

Figure 3A. Homer Dodge Martin, *Honfleur Light*, 1890–92. Oil on canvas, 23 × 36 (sight) in. This is the original picture for the photograph in fig. 3 which was obtained from Dr. Jonathan Harding, Curator, at the Century Assocation and is being published courtesy of the Century Association. It is interesting to note the differences between a photograph and the actual image.

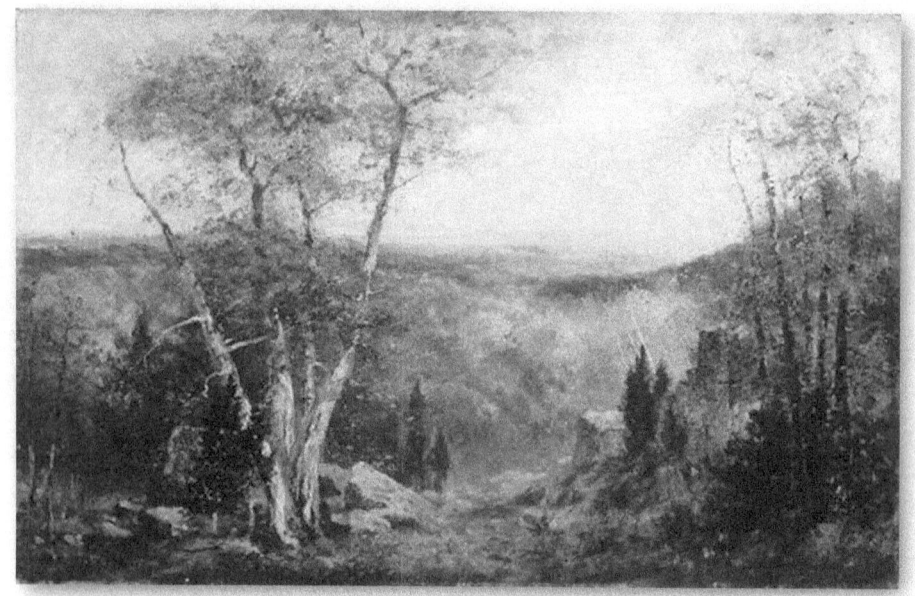

Figure 4. Homer Dodge Martin, *In the Adirondacks*, 1881. Oil on canvas, 30.8 cm × 48.6 cm. Detroit Institute of Arts, Michigan

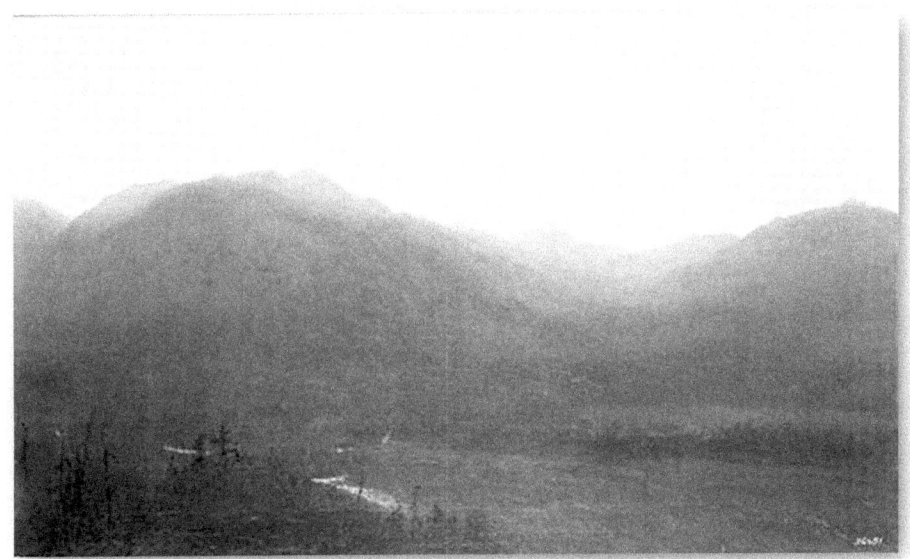

Figure 5. Homer Dodge Martin, *Ausable Valley and Mt. Marcy*, YEAR. Oil on canvas, 16 1/4 × 26 1/2 in. Presented by the artist as initiation fee, in 1866, to the Century Association, New York. Courtesy of the Century Association.

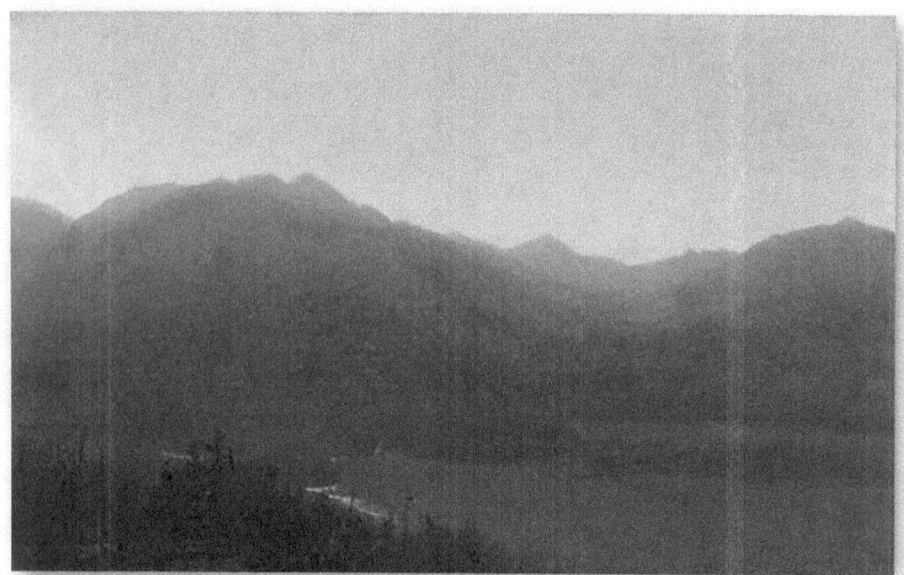

Figure 5A. Homer Dodge Martin, *Ausable Valley and Mt. Marcy*, YEAR. Oil on canvas, 16 1/4 × 26 1/2 in. Presented by the artist as initiation fee, in 1866, to the Century Association, New York. This is the original picture for the photograph in fig. 5, which was obtained from Dr. Jonathan Harding, Curator, at the Century Assocation and is being published courtesy of the Century Association. It is interesting to note the differences between a photograph and the actual image.

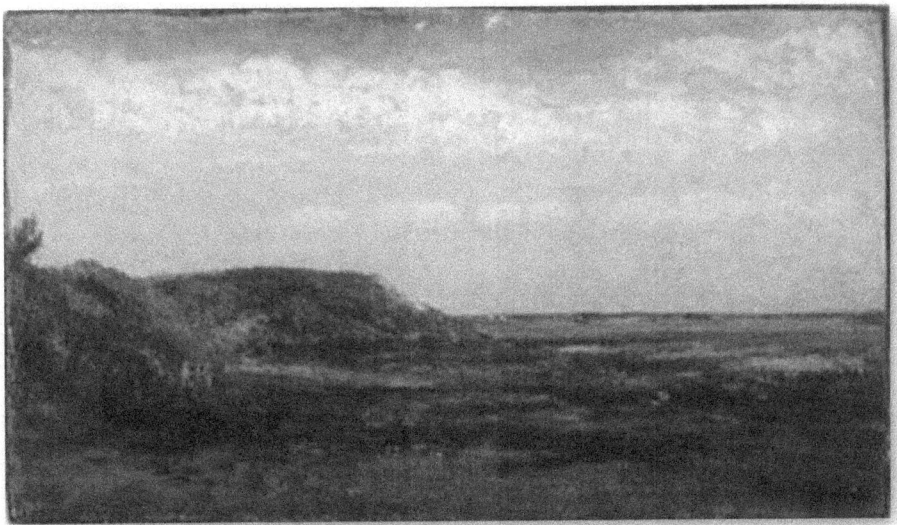

Figure 6. Homer Dodge Martin, *Normandy Coast*, 1884. Oil on board, 7 3/16 × 12 11/16 in. (18.3 × 32.2 cm). Brooklyn Museum, New York. In about 1870, Martin began to shed the early influence of the Hudson River School on his art in favor of the less detailed and looser manner of the French Barbizon school, an informal network of mid-nineteenth-century artists who practiced plein-air painting in the Forest of Fontainebleau, near Barbizon. Martin himself sketched around Barbizon in 1876 and later returned to France for an extended stay in Villerville, where he executed remarkably fresh, freely brushed outdoor paintings such as this.

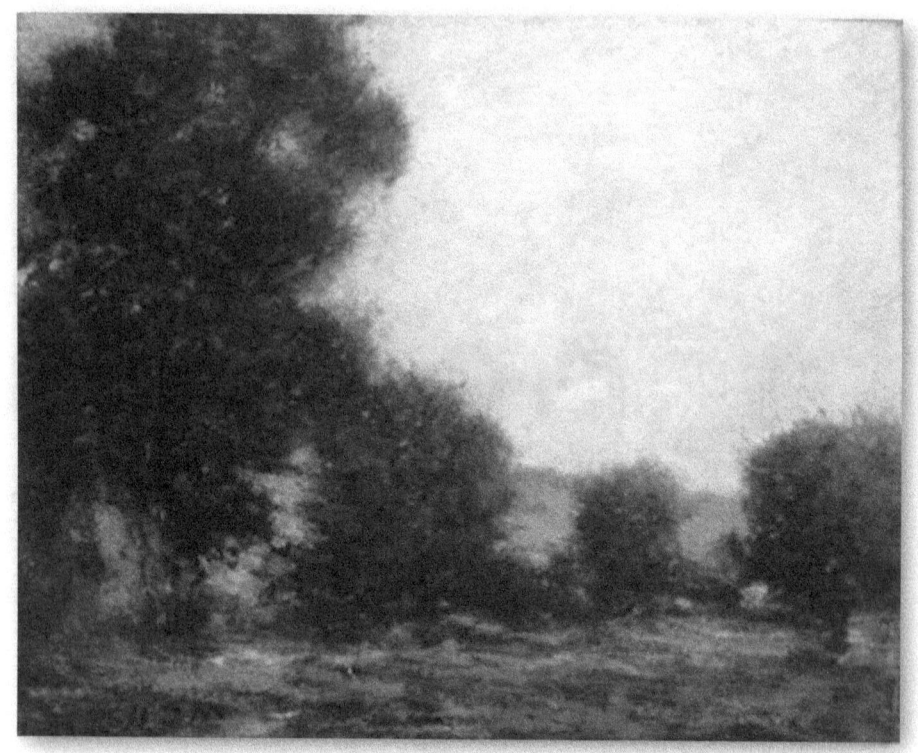

Figure 7. Homer Dodge Martin, *Effect of Trees*, ca. 1879. Oil on canvas, 8 1/16 × 10 1/16 in. (20.5 × 25.6 cm). Brooklyn Museum, New York.

Signature: Signed lower left: "H D M"
The Brooklyn Museum
Credit Line: Gift of Daniel and Rita Fraad, Jr.

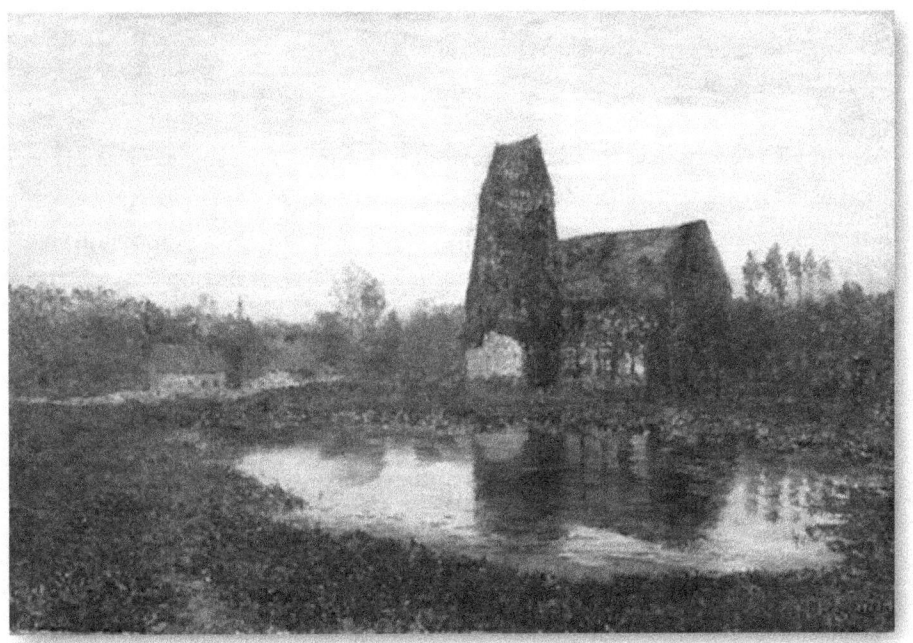

Figure 8. Homer Dodge Martin, *Criqueboeuf Church, Normandy*, 1893. Oil on canvas, 25 1/2 × 38 in. (64.7 × 96.5 cm), Los Angeles County Museum of Art, California.

Alexander Helwig Wyant: Overcoming Physical Disability in Pursuit of His Art

Alexander Helwig Wyant (fig. 1) was born in 1836, the same year as Homer Dodge Martin. With Ralph Albert Blakelock, these three artists were the last of the Hudson River School, using landscape to express grandeur, emotion, and spirituality. Over the course of its history, the Hudson River School, although ever concerned with landscape, had mutated and grown. Wyant, Martin and Blakelock used tone and color to express emotions and meanings in their work rather than simply portray a photographic replica of an image. They are considered American tonalists, fitting in between Barbizon and impressionism. All three are considered indigenous American artists, although Homer did travel to Europe for prolonged visits, and Wyant went to study in Dusseldorf and then visited England and Ireland.

Wyant was a remarkable man who led a courageous and determined life. He was raised in a small farming town in Ohio, where he spent his childhood barefoot and being educated in a one-room school. On his own, he determined to become an artist and worked at his craft diligently from childhood onward. Seeing a few paintings by George Inness, he went to New York to visit and consult with him. He went to Europe to study but understood that the art there was not his style; he was confident enough to reject the teachings of the older artists. He fell in love with one of his art students and married her. Always frail and in poor health, Wyant was a sketch artist on a military expedition to the Southwest when he suffered a stroke, which paralyzed his right arm and then his entire right side. He was not deterred, proceeding to learn to paint with his left hand. Never socially comfortable, he gradually withdrew from life, living in his home in the Catskills and painting continually. Toward the end of his life, his paralysis caused him to walk with a sideways shuffle, but it never stopped him from pursuing and improving his art.

THE ARTIST'S LIFE

Alexander Helwig Wyant was born on January 11, 1836, in Evans Creek, Ohio, his mother's hometown. His father was from Pennsylvania and worked as a farmer and sometimes a carpenter. Wyant's middle name, Helwig, is his maternal grandmother's Dutch maiden name.[83] Shortly after his birth, the family moved to Defiance, Ohio, where he went to the village school.[84] Defiance was near a very unhealthy marshland, appropriately called the Black Swamp, which may have contributed to the poor health that plagued Wyant his whole life.[85] Wyant was the typical barefoot boy, growing up in a small former frontier town with a population, prior to the Civil War, of less than a thousand people. The education he received consisted of little more than basic reading, writing, and arithmetic. He then started apprenticing with a harness and saddle maker and in his late teens became a sign maker.[86] With no apparent encouragement, just of his own volition, Wyant decided at a young age to become an artist.[87] His earliest dated and signed painting is from 1854, when he was eighteen.[88]

Cincinnati at the time was the principal art center of the West. Anecdotally, a distinguished New York artist is said to have visited the Ohio city and encountered Wyant's pictures exhibited in a second-rate print shop. The work was so unlike anything he had seen that he arranged a meeting with Wyant,

---

83 Robert Spencer Olpin, "Alexander Helwig Wyant (1836–1892), American Landscape Painter: An Investigation of His Life and Fame with a Critical Analysis of His Word with a Catalogue Raisonné of Wyant Paintings" (PhD diss., Boston University Graduate School, 1971), 73.

84 Eliot Candee Clark, *Alexander Wyant* (New York: privately printed, 1916), 9.

85 Olpin, "Alexander Helwig Wyant," 76.

86 Ibid., 79.

87 John C. Van Dyke, *American Painting and Its Tradition* (New York: Charles Scribner's Sons, 1919), 46.

88 Olpin, "Alexander Helwig Wyant," 80.

whom he found hard at work but crude in his ideas on art and "as uncultivated as a backwoodsman."[89]

On a visit to Cincinnati in 1857, twenty-one-year-old Wyant saw some paintings by George Inness, which prompted this small-town boy who had never left Ohio to take the long trip to New York to visit Inness and consult with the elder artist about his career. Afterward, he returned to Cincinnati and devoted himself to his painting. Inness had located a patron for Wyant in Cincinnati: Nicholas Longworth, Ohio's leading capitalist and a supporter of the arts.[90] In 1863, he moved to New York to further his career. In 1864 Wyant was shown in a National Academy exhibition and the very next year sailed to Europe to further his education in Düsseldorf. He had seen the work of Hans Gude, a Norwegian artist who was teaching in Carlsruhe, and became his student. In the 1860s, artists were not expressing pessimistic feelings about nature or depicting it as menacing, so it was a revelation to Wyant to see Gude's paintings that the North Sea seem alien to man.[91] Unfortunately, that kind of inspiration was not truly what he was seeking: Wyant was already looking for a more personal form of expression, and Gude's hauntingly majestic mountains and waterfalls did not suit his needs.[92]

Before returning to America, Wyant visited England and Ireland, where he was overwhelmed by John Constable, whom he could relate to and understand. Constable painted the landscape in his vicinity, as "a kingdom of his own," which he loved. Although Turner was a more successful artist, Wyant found his work too visionary, romantic, and overly emotional and the colors too intense and unnatural. The old masters did not appeal to him, either. Wyant was a "reticent and unassuming young man" from a small country town who wished to show the "natural charm of his native land."[93]

---

89   "American Painters: Alexander H. Wyant, N. A.," *Art Journal (1875–1880)*, n.s., 2 (1886): 353–56, http://www.jstor.org/stable/20568990..

90   Olpin, "Alexander Helwig Wyant," 84.

91   James Thomas Flexner, *That Wilder Image: The Painting of America's Native School from Thomas Cole to Winslow Homer* (New York: Little, Brown, 1962), 324–25.

92   Van Dyke, *American Painting and Its Tradition*, 49.

93   Clark, *Alexander Wyant*, 11.

In 1866 Wyant established his studio at 58 West 57th Street in New York, where he remained until 1873, and became a close friend of Inness, who was in New York from 1866 to 1873.[94] Wyant was elected an associate of the National Academy in 1868 and, based upon his painting *The Upper Susquehanna*, a full member in 1869. His paintings were exhibited no fewer than thirty-two times during this period. He still struggled to make a living, and in 1873 joined a military expedition to Arizona and New Mexico as a sketch artist. The trip would give him an opportunity to study nature and be out of doors. Unfortunately, Wyant had never been in great health: exposure, fatigue, and lack of proper food proved too much for him, causing complete exhaustion and illness. He was sent back to New York by train. Although the route passed by Defiance, Ohio, where his mother was still living, he chose to go on to New York, where, although he had few friends, his career was anchored.[95] The illness resulted in a stroke that paralyzed his right side and painting arm. The west not only maimed him physically but taught him nothing artistically. Undeterred, he learned to paint with his left hand.[96]

Always a shy man, this disability made him even more introspective and taciturn. A neighbor told Clark that although he perhaps knew Wyant better than any other person, he still knew very little about him. Wyant never spoke much, which made him seem gruff and uncivil. By the late 1870s, Wyant's style began to grow broader and simpler each year, appealing more to the collecting public and making him more prosperous. He was able to maintain a studio at the YMCA building at 23rd Street in New York and attracted students.[97] The landscape painter Bruce Crane became a student of Wyant's in 1879. He was given a key to the studio, told to enter at will, and entrusted with the principal task of simply copying Wyant's paintings, with Wyant giving little advice in words.[98]

---

94 Olpin, "Alexander Helwig Wyant," 91.

95 Van Dyke, *American Painting and Its Tradition*, 53.

96 Clark, *Alexander Wyant*, 13.

97 Van Dyke, *American Painting and Its Tradition*, 54

98 Clark, *Alexander Wyant*, 29–30.

Wyant was accepted for membership in the Society of American Artists in 1878 and became a founding member of the American Watercolor Society as well as the Century Association.[99] In 1880, Wyant married his pupil Arabella Locke, who went on to become a respected watercolor painter. They had one son. They spent their summers in Keene Valley and in 1889 purchased a home in the town of Arkville, deep in the Catskill Mountains in New York State. A small porch was built on the western side of the house, which allowed a panoramic view of the scenery; from there, Wyant unceasingly painted, generating numerous pictures. He was successful in the sale of his paintings but always seemed rather indifferent. He was too absorbed in their production to concern himself with their sale.[100]

With their sense of melancholy and sadness, Wyant's paintings were referred to as "sentimental landscapes" and would have been considered morbid by the traditional Hudson River painters. Collectors of the day found these paintings extremely satisfactory, and the slowly dying man, living in agony, was besieged with praise and orders. His art does point "to the more powerful crepuscular landscapes of Ralph Albert Blakelock," who was actively painting but receiving little recognition.[101]

Living almost as a hermit in his isolated mountain home, Wyant continued to paint and to improve his technique.[102] As time progressed, the paralysis spread from his right arm through his entire right side. He was always in great pain. He would walk sideways, shuffling his feet. Despite these physical issues, he continued to paint, almost to the point of exhaustion. He died on November 29, 1892.[103]

THE ARTIST'S STYLE AND WORK

Wyant's early period can be defined as the ten years leading up to his illness and stroke in 1873. In his paintings, Wyant was not concerned about bright,

99 Van Dyke, *American Painting and Its Tradition*, 55

100 Clark, *Alexander Wyant*, 31–32.

101 Flexner, *That Wilder Image*, 327.

102 Van Dyke, *American Painting and Its Tradition*, 46.

103 Ibid., 32.

clear, sunny days. As in Constable's work, the sky was usually overcast, with the moving clouds indicating the spirit of change. With a large expatriate artistic community, Düsseldorf had become a mecca for American artists. Wyant went to see and learn, and although he did not find the approach fully agreeable, he did fall under its influence. His paintings during this period had a great photographic fidelity to nature: emphasis is on the scenic interest and its natural beauty, at the expense of the proper arrangement and balance of forms and color. Wyant understood that this approach was too superficial to produce great or noble art. The significant detail included in paintings by the Düsseldorf school was greatly appreciated by collectors, who could study the details under a magnifying glass.[104]

Wyant would use the same technique in painting both his large and small pictures. All had great detail, which can be seen in comparing the small *Keene Valley* (fig. 4) with the much larger *Mohawk Valley* (fig. 5). In emphasizing detail, each part of the painting is considered as carefully, as "effect." Volume and simplicity are lost. As he developed, Wyant was able to move forward and build on this understanding.[105] Interestingly, in 1866, the same year that *Mohawk Valley* (fig. 5) was completed, Wyant painted an Irish landscape, *View in County Kerry, Ireland* (fig. 3), which is remarkable for its simplicity of composition, absent small objects and distracting details. Both pictures are in the Metropolitan Museum of Art in New York. It would appear that he painted *Mohawk Valley* (fig. 5) before sailing abroad and being influenced by Constable.[106] Flexner reads *Mohawk Valley* as the prototype for many of his future paintings. Instead of closing off the picture with mountains, Wyant fills half the canvas with sky. The air is painted with a luminosity that reflects Constable's use of sky.[107] Over his lifetime, Wyant painted many pictures of the area surrounding the Mohawk Valley, such as *An Old Cearing* (fig. 6).

---

104 Ibid., 16–18.
105 Ibid., 18–20.
106 Van Dyke, *American Painting and Its Tradition*, 50–51.
107 Flexner, *That Wilder Image*, 325–26.

Wyant also started by using a very restricted palette of neutral colors and grays. Along with his close observation of nature, this palette was able to produce a "sensitive appreciation of light" that allowed his personal observations to become more pronounced. He used a diffused light, where the sun is shielded behind overhanging clouds, casting a "veiled radiance over the landscape." Wyant also learned to work out of doors, as the German painters did in order to study the forms and details of particular objects rather than to obtain an impression, at a particular time, of light and atmosphere. Good examples are *Landscape* (fig. 10), painted in 1865, and *Tennessee* (fig. 9), painted in 1866, which are almost photographic in their vision, lacking both selection and distinction.[108] All this changed as Wyant became prepared to sacrifice details for simplicity and aesthetic composition.

In the late 1870s, Wyant became very interested in the style of the Barbizon painters. He even sent to the National Academy for exhibition a picture he entitled *In the Spirit of Rousseau*. When told by a dealer that his pictures were "very much like the Barbizon men," he was extremely pleased.[109] Both the Barbizon painters and the late Hudson River School painters, such as Wyant, Inness, and Martin, began to see nature as a reflection of the soul and took a pantheistic approach to it. Being forced now to use his left hand, Wyant began to see that a certain generalization of form gave a greater simplicity of effect, thereby allowing him to express something more than facts. Neither his work nor that of the Barbizon painters could not bare the same magnifying glass examination of minute details which the Düsseldorf school had provided.[110] In 1876, a critic described Wyant as rarely composing his images but rather studying and selecting his views from nature with the object of working on them at his leisure. This method usually produced striking pictures.[111]

The transition to painting with his left hand was greatly facilitated by Inness's later work as well as by the flood of Barbizon paintings that were

---

108 Van Dyke, *American Painting and Its Tradition*, 19–23.
109 Ibid., 30–31.
110 Ibid., 34–35.
111 "American Painters," 354.

being brought to America. It encouraged him to give up producing large vistas, which were too arduous for him to paint, and instead to focus on more intimate views, similar to the Barbizon paintings.[112] The charcoal drawing *Landscape* (fig. 11) is a good example of this.

This approach was a revelation for Wyant. He could be more sympathetic in his appreciation, and he could render a more intimate response to nature. Mass and values became more important than accurate details. This approach was perfect for his use of diffused sunlight through clouds as illusive suggestions, as opposed to a literal and photographic attention to facts. This became evident in Wyant's reduction of the angle of vision in his paintings, thereby concentrating the eyes in one area alone. He began to do more and more work out of doors.[113]

Although working with only a few neutralized colors on a small palette, Wyant never produced a muddy or unanimated surface. His paintings contain no strong color contrasts. He used small brushes. Being concerned with the diffusion of light, he never created flat surfaces. His pictures are intimate, intended to be viewed across the room, in a home—not to stand out in a large gallery. He understood the use of thinning paint with linseed oil to produce a semitransparent glaze. By applying layers of this glaze, he produced more luminous and richer colors. This is what made him a great tonalist.[114]

Wyant preferred a dark foreground and a lighted middle distance with a veiled sunlight effect in the back. He avoided the obviousness of this sort of composition by introducing such elements as light spots from a pool in the dark foreground and dark tree trunks and stumps in the lighted middle distance, always seeking to vary the contrast of light and dark. Until he became too ill, Wyant preferred painting out of doors and placing the images he saw directly onto the canvas:[115] "Much of his work was melancholy and lassitudinous. Showing at its most typical the fall of night from overcast skys. . . .

---

112 Flexner, *That Wilder Image*, 326.

113 Clark, *Alexander Wyant*, 35–45.

114 Ibid., 50–53.

115 Van Dyke, *American Painting and Its Tradition*, 60–61.

expressing the relief mixed with sadness that the day's end brings to an invalid whose day has been full of pain."[116]

Clark reports that Wyant often remarked that if one could paint the sky, one could paint a landscape. In truth, in many of Wyant's paintings, it is the sky that is of dominant interest. Wyant also liked to show distance in his paintings. These are the two primary factors that induced him to his usual practice of placing the horizon line below the center of the canvas. Cloud formations are a major factor in the composition of paintings that are dominated by the sky. Constable knew this well and was also careful in depicting his clouds. It is part of Wyant's genius that the sky always belongs to the landscape. The artist also enjoyed playing with the shadows that these clouds cast on the world beneath. He does enhance these scenes with the use of chiaroscuro. Wyant was careful to balance the spatial relationships of this light and dark to produce the restful scenes that make these pictures so appealing.[117]

Olpin is correct in describing Wyant's career as moving from early luminism in the style of the Hudson River School toward a total impressionism with the sensibilities of Constable, to the French Barbizon painters, and then to the later style of George Inness.[118]

Isham regarded Wyant as painting "variations on a single note." He regards his typical picture as "a glimpse of sunny, rolling country seen between the trunks of trees that have grown tall and slender in a wood, usually birches and maples." He did like the exactness with which Wyant modeled clouds, with his firm brushstrokes, without losing the "sentiment and silvery shimmer" that defined his work. He compared Wyant to Inness in that both "altered and matured their style" with a "steady subjective development." Isham regarded Homer Dodge Martin as a far better artist.[119]

Wyant was interested in form over color. He used shadow and soft light to bring out these forms. He was moving in the direction opposite of the impressionists'. Wyant was concerned with portraying the material world as spiritual

---

116 Flexner, *That Wilder Image*, 327.
117 Clark, *Alexander Wyant*, 55–64.
118 Olpin, "Alexander Helwig Wyant," abstract.
119 Samuel Isham, *The History of American Painting* (New York: Macmillan, 1936), 261–62.

substance. In many ways, he represented an older tradition that had been cast aside in the search for the new. He did not use large-scale images, bright colors, or gaudy images to attract attention. Like his pictures, he was always shy and of few words. He sought to continue his work rather than attract attention. It is our duty to remember those who could never speak for themselves.

POSTHUMOUS PRICE HISTORY OF THE ARTIST'S PAINTINGS

Olpin, who has written probably the only doctoral thesis on Wyant, writes about the existing literature on the artist. Independent research for the present project, although not as rigorous as his, confirms Olpin's findings. Wyant seems to have gained most of his popularity in the first two decades of the twentieth century. Thereafter, the amount of information steadily diminishes, all but disappearing after the mid-1930s.[120] Although not particularly comprehensive or organized, Eliot Candee Clark's biography of Wyant, privately published in 1916 and cited extensively herein, seems to be the only single book about Wyant. Olpin's doctoral thesis, on the other hand, is simply superb, well organized, comprehensive and a true model for all future researchers in nineteenth-century American art.

Wyant is known to have destroyed a number of his early works as he changed styles.[121] After his death, his wife is reported to have also destroyed many of his paintings, for the purpose of maintaining a high standard of quality. Wyant did not date most of his paintings, so time frames must be established based on style.

In reviewing the auction of the Clarke collection at Chickering Hall in 1899, Skalet reports that Wyant's *Dawn-Keene Valley* sold for $2,500 ($72,400). She goes on to note that it was predicted that Clarke's pictures would sell for far higher prices than previously paid for contemporary American artists.[122]

---

120 Ibid., x.

121 Ibid., xxvii.

122 Linda Skalet, "Thomas B. Clarke, American Collector," *Archives of the American Art Journal* 15, no. 3 (1975): 2–7, http://www.jstor.org/stable/1557068.

In the 1900 sale of the Estate of William L. Picknell at the Fifth Avenue Art Galleries in New York, the "splendid" *In the Adirondacks* by Wyant was sold to George A. Hearn for $6,300 ($180,000). The author of an article on the sale was careful to note that Inness and Martin were stronger painters than Wyant.[123] In a 1912 article, a critic quoting a letter from William T. Evans notes that *In the Adirondacks* is now worth $30,000 ($743,000) and that *Connecticut Valley*, purchased before Wyant's death for $1,800 ($51,500), is now insured by the Lotus Club for $20,000 ($496,000). In addition, *No Man's Land* (fig. 2) was purchased at the Clarke sale in 1899 for $550 ($15,900) and recently sold for $6,500 ($161,000) at the Bonner sale.[124]

In a 1904 interview with Thomas E. Kirby of the American Art Association, a review of his firm's auction records indicated that he had auctioned a total of forty-five Wyant paintings over the years. In 1887 a 15 × 13" painting sold for $75.00 ($1,890). In 1891, at the Seney Sale, three were sold as follows: 15 × 12" at $450 ($11,900), 18 × 30" at $650 ($17,200) and 16 × 20" at $750 ($19,800). In 1899 at the Clarke sale, a 20 × 30" sold at $1,200 ($34,800), and an 18 × 30" at $2,500 ($72,400). In 1900 at the Evans sale, a 26 × 40" sold for $2,550 ($73,000), and a 37 × 50" at $6,500 ($186,000).[125] *Broad, Silent Valley* (fig. 7) and *Glimpse of the Sea* (fig. 8) are typical of his works that were in demand at the time.

This study of the posthumous price history of Wyant's paintings starts from 1946, when a new generation of collectors, critics, and scholars came on the scene in the aftermath of World War II. Pricing will be based from 1946 to 1984 on *World Collectors Annuary*[126] (almost all auctions cited being from Parke-Bernet), and from 1986 to 2014 on Artnet.[127] For ease of comparison, equivalent current

---

123 "New York Art," *Brush and Pencil* 5, no. 6 (1900): 270–73, http://www.jstor.org/stable/25505523.

124 "Two Great Artists: Inness and Wyant," *Fine Arts Journal*, 27, no. 4 (1912): 673–76, http://jstor.org/stable/25587149.

125 "Appreciation in Value of American Paintings," *Brush and Pencil* 14, no. 1 (1904): 14–15, http://www.jstor.org/stable/25540488.

126 A. M. E. Van Eijk Van Voorthusijen, ed., *World Collectors Annuary* (Delft, Netherlands: Brouwer, n.d.).

127 Artnet price database, accessed February 23, 2015, https://www.artnet.com/price-database/.

prices are placed in parentheses.[128] When more than five paintings were sold at auction in any year, the highest price is listed, followed by the range of high and low prices for the remainder. There are sometimes large time gaps but it is not clear whether this is due to no auction sales having occurred or simple clerical omissions.

1946

Forest at Sunset, 10 ½ × 14 ¼", from Joseph G. Snydacker, New York $100 ($1,190)

1950

A River Scene, 19 1/2 × 35 ½" Parke Bernet 52.10 Britsh Pounds ($1,970)

1951

Early Morn, 37 × 49" from Emerson McMillan, New York 1913 and from 1899 Clarke sale $200 ($1,790)

1956

Fornoon in the Adirondacks, 33 × 42 ¾" from The Metropolitan Museum of Art, New York $850 ($7,290)

1967

Landscape, 20 × 30" $1,700 ($11,900)

1968

Woodland Scene, The Adirondacks, 25 × 19" $3,300 ($22,100)

---

128 Measuring Worth, accessed February 23, 2015, http://measuringworth.com/uscompare.

1969

Cloudy Day, 12 ½ × 18" $1,300 ($8,260)
Landscape, 16 × 12 ½" $600 ($3,810)
Summer Landscape, 20 × 30" $1,500 ($9,530)

1970

The Mouth of the Ausable River $10,000 ($60,000)

1971

Passing Clouds, 39 × 49" from Emerson McMillan and included in Eliot Clark's 1919 book $6000 ($34,500)

1972

Autumn Woods, 12 × 16" $1,500 ($8,350)
Grey Morning, 16 ¼ × 20" from William Barkentine, New York $700 ($3,900)
In the Rocky Pasture, 18 ½ × 23 ¼" $2,300 ($12,800)
In the Catskills, 17 × 23" from Childs Gallery, Boston $7,000 ($39,000)

1973

Sun in Kentucky, 16 1/2 × 27 ½" 1100 British Pounds ($16,800)
Summer Pasture, 20 × 16" $800 ($4,190)
Woodland Glade, 15 × 39.5 cm. $2,250 ($11,800)

1974

Landscape, 51.4 × 76.6 cm. $1,900 ($8,970)
Adirondack Vista, 24 1/2 × 18 ½" from William T. Evans and included in Eliot Clark's 1920 book $2,900 ($13,700)

1975

Landscape in the Adirondacks, 76.5 × 63.4 cm. $2,000 ($8,650)
Landscape on a Foggy Day, 66 × 101.6 cm. $4,000 ($17,300)

1976

Mouth of the Ausable River, 14 3/4 × 25" $12,000 ($49,100)

1977

Mountain Landscape, 18 1/4 × 14 ¼" $2,200 ($8,460)
Near Arkville, New York, 11 3/4 × 16" Exhibited at the Montclair Art Museum $1,700 ($6,530)
Summer Afternoon, 25 × 28 ½" $5,250 ($20,200)

1978

Lake Scene, 14 1/4 × 20" $6,000 ($21,400)
Newport Landscape, 8 × 14" $3,000 ($10,700)

1981

Rising Mist, 10 × 17" Exhibited at Union League Club 1978-79, $14,000 ($35,900)

1985

Sun in Kentucky, 17 × 28" Parke Bernet $20,500 ($44,400)
Woodlan d Stream, 15.9 × 21.9" Christie's New York $4,400 ($9,530)
Sunset, 16.1 × 22" Christie's New York $6,600 ($14,300)

1986
Country Landscape, 5.1 × 9.5" $2,200 ($4,680)

1987
Sunset in the Marshes, 36.9 × 49.1" Christie's New York $12,100 ($24,800)
Country Landscape, 5.1 × 9.5" Christie's New York $2,200 ($4,510)
Resting on the Shore, 9.1 × 14.3" Christie's New York $7,700 ($15,800)
Landscape at Dusk, 24.2 × 30.5" Sotheby's Arcade $1,650 ($3,380)
Woods and Brook, 12 × 16" Christie's New York $3,080 ($6,320)

1988
Evening, 11 × 16.3" Sotheby's Arcade $2,750 ($5,420)

1989
Summer Landscape, 11.8 × 19.2" Sotheby's Arcade $5,500 ($10,300)
Evening, 9.8 × 14" Butterfields $1,650 ($3,100)
Cows Grazing in an Extensive Landscape, 15.4 × 22.1" Sotheby's Arcade
$10,450 ($19,600)

1990
The End of Summer, 28.5 × 35.5" Sotheby's New York $25,300 ($41,900)
Six other paintings by the artist were sold at auction that year, ranging in
prices from $600 ($1,680) to $7,700 (($13,700).

1991
Autumn in Landscape, 18.1 × 30" Christie's New York $22,000 ($37,600)
Astoundingly twelve (12) other paintings by the artist were sold at auction
that year ranging in price from $660 ($1,130) to $9,500 ($16,200).

1992

A Path to the River, 22.4 × 30.1" Christie's New York $8,800 ($14,600)
Nine (9) other paintings by the artist were sold at auction that year ranging in price from $385 ($639) to $3,575 ($5,940).

1993

Summer Haunt, 36.5 × 48.5" Sotheby's New York $35,650 ($57,500)
Again, nine (9) other paintings by the artist were sold at auction that year, ranging in price from $770 ($1,240) to $21,850 ($35,200).

1994

Landscape Scene, 22.2 × 28.5" Skinner $3,220 ($5,060)
Rocky Stream, Early Summer, 32.2 × 25.2" C.G. Sloan $5,250 ($8,250)
Cow Watering in a Wooded Landscape, 11 × 8.3" Doyle New York $575 ($904)
Evening, 11 × 16.1" C.G. Sloan $1,700 ($2,670)

1995

Summer Silence, 35.2 × 28.3" Sotheby's New York $13,800 ($21,100)
Ten (10) other paintings by the artist were sold at auction that year ranging in price from $1,250 ($1,910) to $9,516 ($14,500). Interestingly two (2) paintings were sold by a French-Canadian auction house in Montreal.

1996

Mount Washington Valley, 14 × 22" Sotheby's New York $28,750 ($42,700)
Another eleven (11) paintings by the artist were sold that year, ranging in price from $700 ($1,040) to $10,925 ($16,200).

1997

Pond in Tonalist Pastoral Landscape, 20 × 30" John Moran Auctioneers $5,500
($7,980)
Six (6) other of the artist's paintings were sold that year at auction, ranging in
price from $750 ($1,090) to $4,025 ($5,840).

1998

Silver Creek, 16 × 24" Weschler's $5,750 ($8,220)
Another five (5) of the artist's paintings were sold that year at auction ranging
in price from $1,150 ($1,640) to $4,370 ($6,250).

1999

View of the Valley, 13.3 × 21" Sotheby's New York $25,300 ($35,460)
Another eight (8) of the artist's paintings were sold at auction that year, ranging in price from $2,400 ($3,360) to $13,000 ($18,200).

2000

Marsh Landscape, 35.7 × 55.5" Christie's Los Angeles $18,800 ($25,400)
Another ten (10) of the artist's paintings were sold that year, ranging in price
from $2,070 ($2,800) to $9,200 ($12,400). One of his paintings was sold at
Koller Auktionen in Berlin.

2001

Farmhouse in a River Valley, 18.5 × 24.5" Sotheby's New York $32,375
($42,600)
Another nine (9) of the artist's paintings were sold that year at auction, ranging in price from $$2,350 ($3,090) to $30,650 ($40,300).

2002

In the Keene Valley, New York, 14.1 × 22.2" Phillips, de Pury & Luxemboug, New York $112,000 ($145,000)
Another eight (8) paintings of the artist were sold at auction that year, ranging in price from $2,530 ($3,280) to $41,400 ($53,600).

2003

Storm Ahead, 22.8 × 31.7" Sotheby's New York $45,000 ($57,000)
Another eleven (11) paintings by the artist were sold at auction that year, ranging in price from $700 ($886) to $33,000 ($41,800).

2004

Mohawk Valley (View of Mt. Tom), 4.5 × 7" Sloans & Kenyon $2,300 ($2,840)
Evening Landscape, 12.2 × 18.2" Shannon's $19,975 ($24,600)
Quiet Stream, 16 × 12" Sloans & Kenyon $2,600 ($3,210)
The Golden Hour, 16 × 12.2" Skinner $14,100 ($17,400)

2005

Storm Over Lake George, 12 × 20" Shannon's $23,900 ($28,500)
Another thirteen (13) paintings by the artist were sold that year, ranging in price from $1,793 ($2,140) to $19,975 ($23,800).

2006

Evening Autumn Landscape, 12 × 16" Christie's New York $21,600 ($25,000)
Another eight (8) of the artist's paintings were sold that year, ranging in price from $359 ($415) to $10,350 ($12,000).

2007

Landscape with Sheep, 17.5 × 14.5" Shannon's $13,200 ($14,800)
Adirondack Creek, 20 × 30" Bonhams New York $10,800 ($12,100)
Hudson River View, 23 × 32" Sotheby's New York $84,000 ($94,400)
The Coming Storm, 15.2 × 25.2" Christie's New York $78,000 ($87,600)
Irish Landscape, 12 × 20" Christie's New York $15,000 ($16,900)

2008

Path to Chapel Pond, 24 × 20.2" Christie's New York $6,250 ($6,760)
Brook in the Woods, 10 × 14" Sotheby's New York $4,375 ($4,730)
Landscape, 14 × 20" Pook & Pook $6,435 ($6,960)
Late Afternoon, 19 × 25.5" Christie's New York $18,750 ($20,300)
Tonalist Landscape, 11.5 × 17.2" Ivey-Selkirk $900 ($974)
Arkville, 13.5 × 19.5" $3,500 ($3790)

2009

A Solitary Horseman, 6.1 × 9.1" Skinner $2,489 ($2,700)
Atmospheric Landscape, 8.2 × 10" John Moran Auctioneers $4,025 ($4,370)
Landscape with Mountains, 18.1 × 30.3" Doyle New York $3,750 ($4,070)
Early Autumn, Adirondacks, 26 × 40" Christie's New York $35,000 ($38,000)

2010

Hudson River View, 23 × 32" Shannon's $96,000 ($103,000)
Six (6) other paintings by the artist were sold that year, ranging in price from
$750 ($801) to $17,850 ($19,100).

2011

Mountain Stream, 13.5 × 18" Leslie Hindman Auctioneers $31,750 ($32,900)

An additional nine (9) paintings by the artist were sold that year, ranging in price from $1,830 ($1,900) to $13,000 ($13,500).

2012

Farmhouse in a River Valley, 18.8 × 24.8" Doyle New York $21,250 ($21,600)
An additional fifteen (15) painting by the artist were sold that year, ranging in price from $850 ($862) to $20,000 ($20,300).

2013

View from the Woods, 28 ¼ × 38 ¼" Heritage Auctions, Texas $20,000
An additional nine (9) paintings by the artist were sold that year, ranging in price from $910 to $4,800.

2014

In the Berkshires, Massachusetts, 20.1 × 24.2" Doyle New York $10,000
An additional twelve (12) paintings by the artist were sold that year, ranging in price from $625 to $8,125.

CONCLUSION

Wyant became more successful after his stroke than he had been before. Throughout his life, his paintings sold well, and at respectable prices. This trend seems to have continued after his death, with his paintings maintaining respectable but not excessive sales prices. His paintings, although mostly very similar, are very appealing and contain a "sensitivity" that raises them above ordinary landscape paintings.

FIGURES

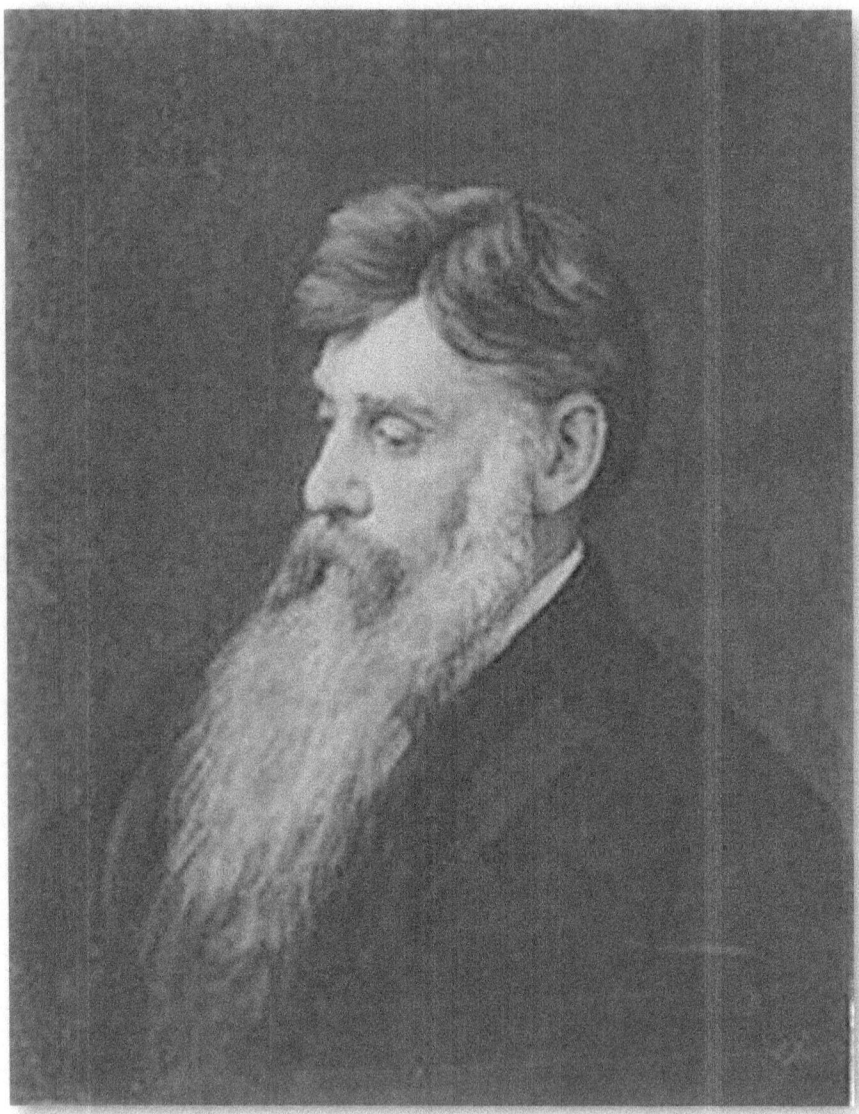

Figure 1. Alexander Helwig Wyant, 1882.Black-and-white photographic print, 22 × 18 cm (photographer unknown). Macbeth Gallery Records, Archives of American Art, Smithsonian Institution, Washington, DC. Accession no. aaa_Macgall_4870.

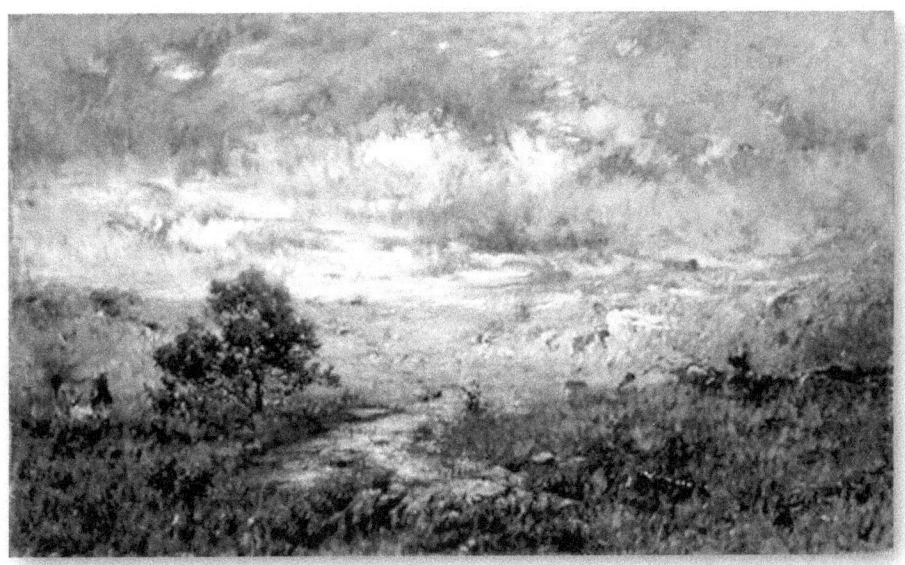

Figure 2. Alexander Helwig Wyant, *Any Man's Land*, before 1880. Oil on canvas, 18 3/16 × 30 in. (46.20 × 76.20 cm). Los Angeles County Museum of Art, California.

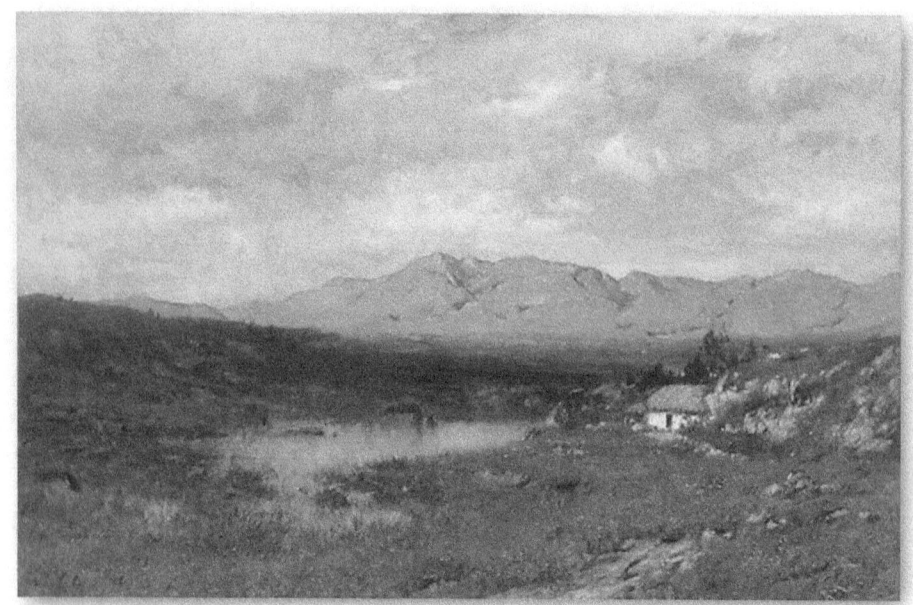

Figure 3. Alexander Helwig Wyant, *View in County Kerry*, ca. 1875.
Oil on canvas, 26 1/4 × 40 in. (66.7 × 101.6 cm). Metropolitan
Museum of Art, New York. Accession no. 87.8.11.

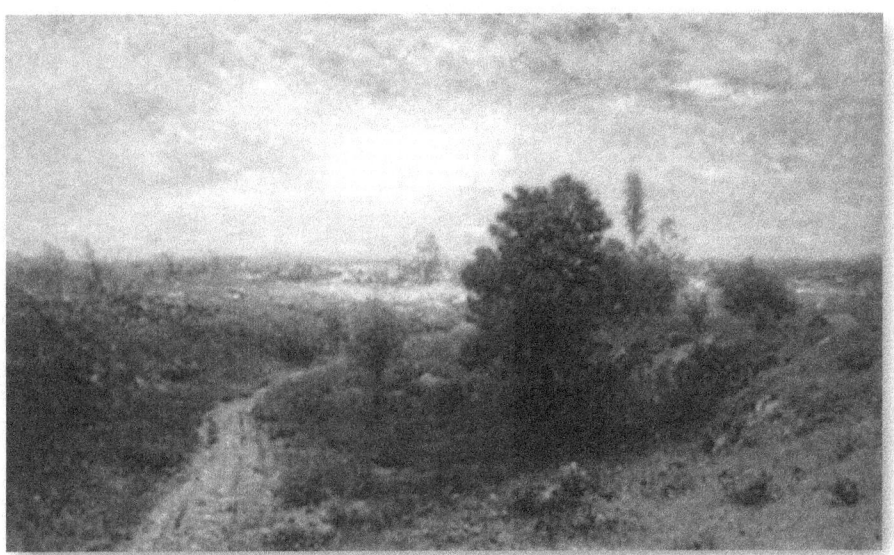

Figure 4. Alexander Helwig Wyant, *Keene Valley*, ca. 1884–86. Oil on canvas, 18 1/16 × 29 15/16 in. (45.8 × 76.1 cm). Brooklyn Museum, New York. Accession no. 13.43.

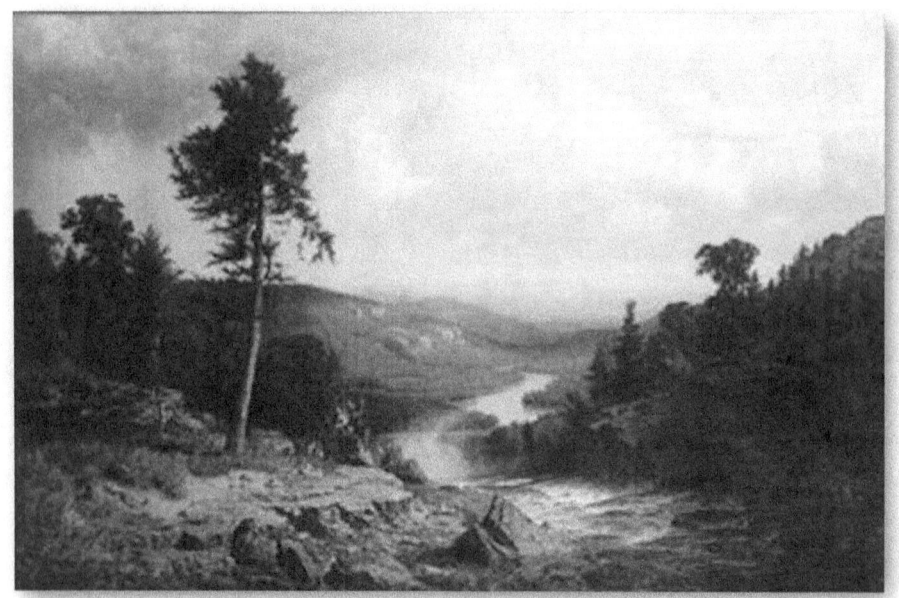

Figure 5. Alexander Helwig Wyant, *The Mohawk Valley*, 1866. Oil on canvas, 34 3/4 × 53 3/4 in. Metropolitan Museum of Art, New York. Gift of Mrs. George E. Schanck in memory of Arthur Hoppock Hearn, 1913. Accession no. 13.53.

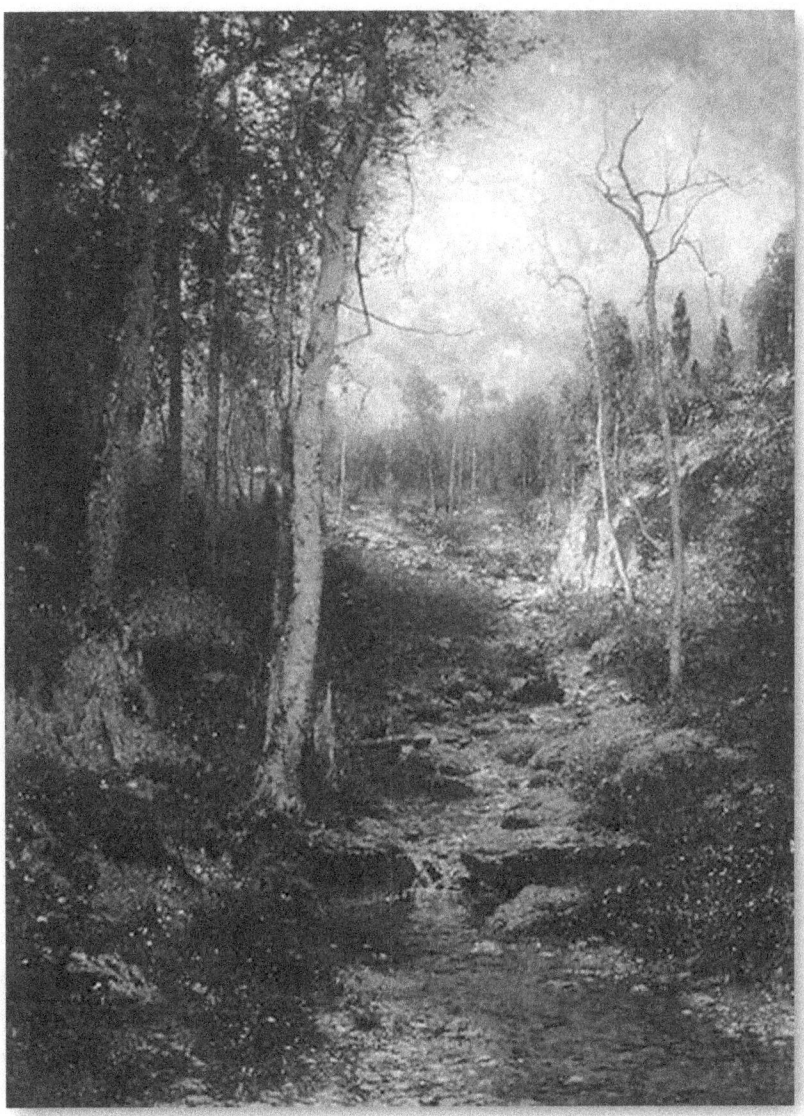

Figure 6. Alexander Helwig Wyant, *An Old Clearing*, 1881. Oil on canvas, 49 1/4 × 37 in. (125.1 × 94 cm). Metropolitan Museum of Art, New York. Gift of Robert Gordon, 1912. Accession no. 12.205.2.

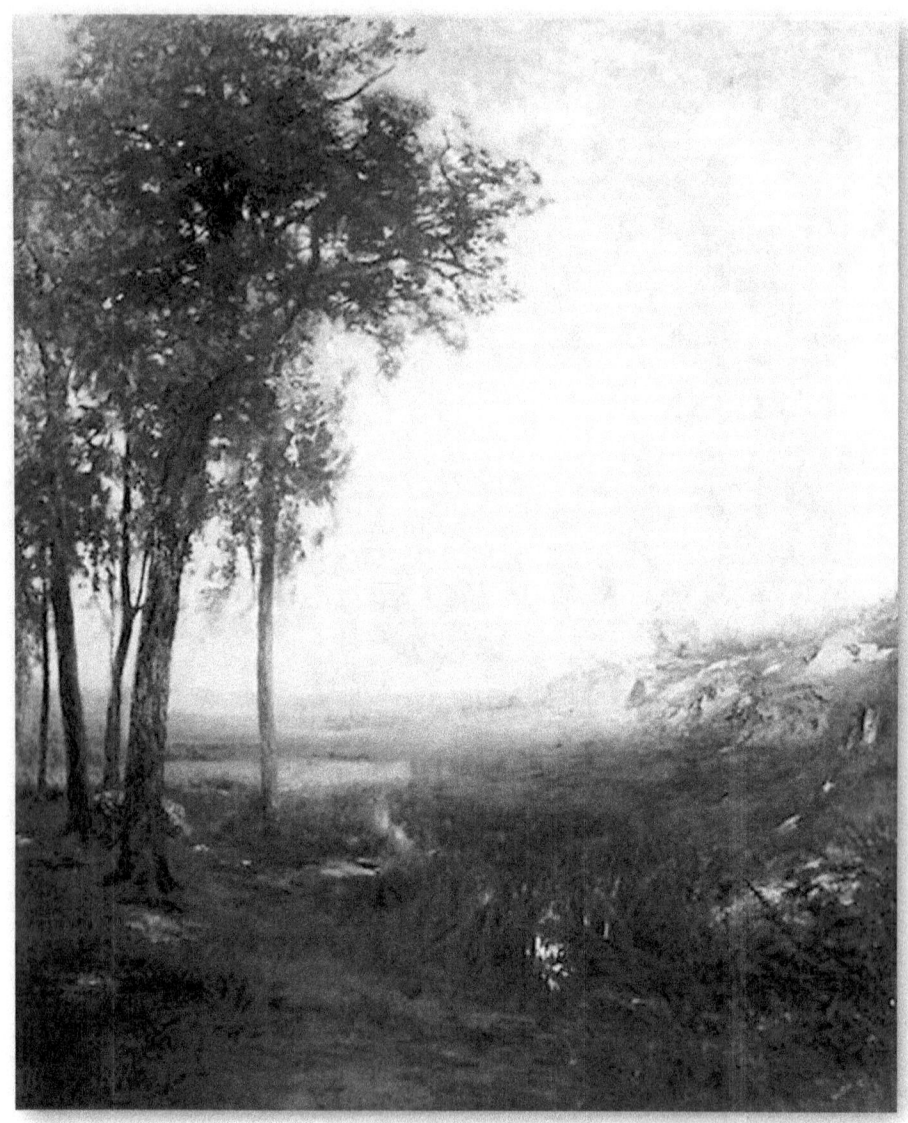

Figure 7. Alexander Helwig Wyant, *Broad, Silent Valley*, ca. 1880–1887. Oil on canvas, 60 5/8 × 50 1/2 in. (154 × 128.3 cm). Metropolitan Museum of Art, New York. Gift of George A. Hearn, 1906. Accession no. 06.1306.

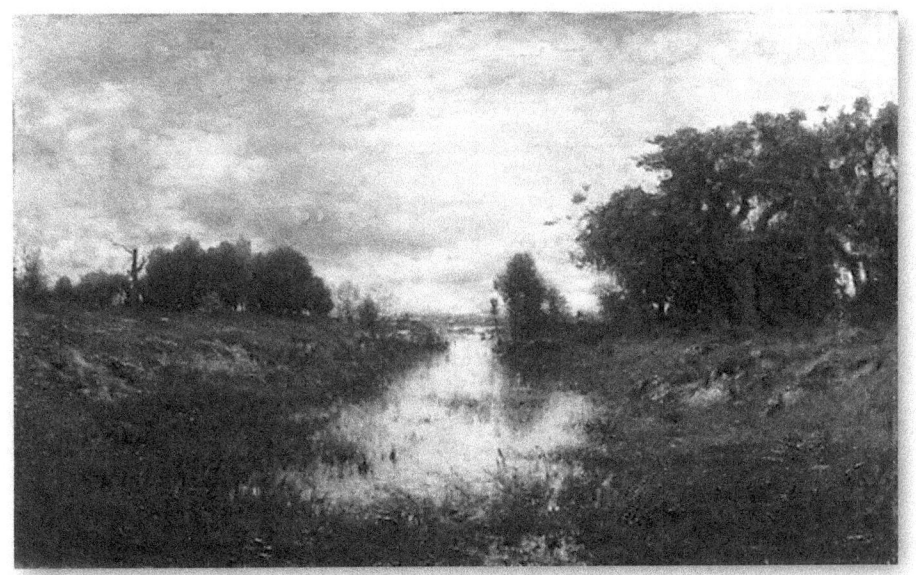

Figure 8. Alexander Helwig Wyant, *Glimpse of the Sea*, 1885. Oil on canvas, 18 1/8 × 30 1/8 in. (46 × 76.5 cm). Metropolitan Museum of Art, New York. Gift of George A. Hearn, 1906. Accession no. 06.1308.

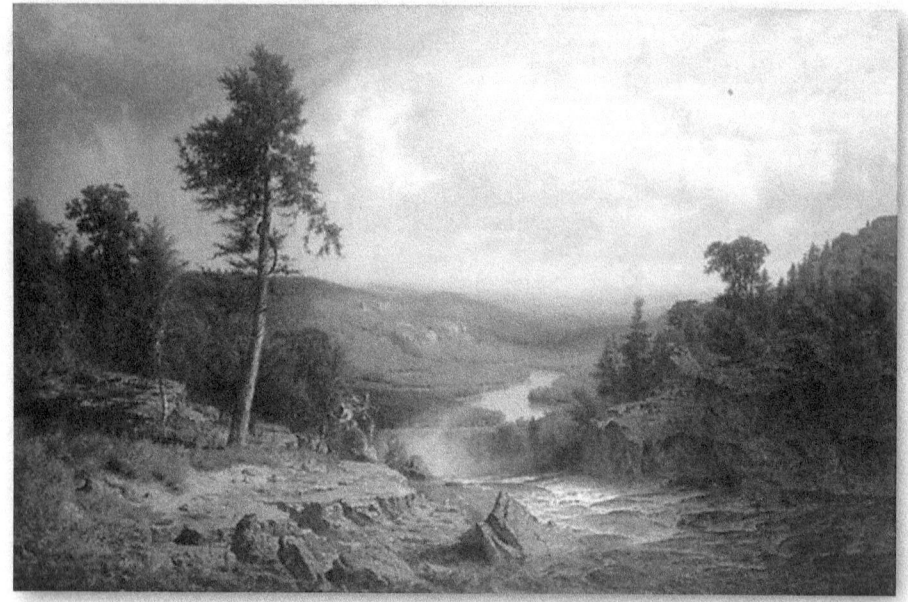

Figure 9. Alexander Helwig Wyant, *Tennessee*, 1866. Oil on canvas, 34 3/4 × 53 3/4 in. (88.3 × 136.5 cm). Metropolitan Museum of Art, New York. Gift of Mrs. George E. Schanck, in memory of her brother, Arthur Hoppock Hearn, 1913. Accession no. 13.53.

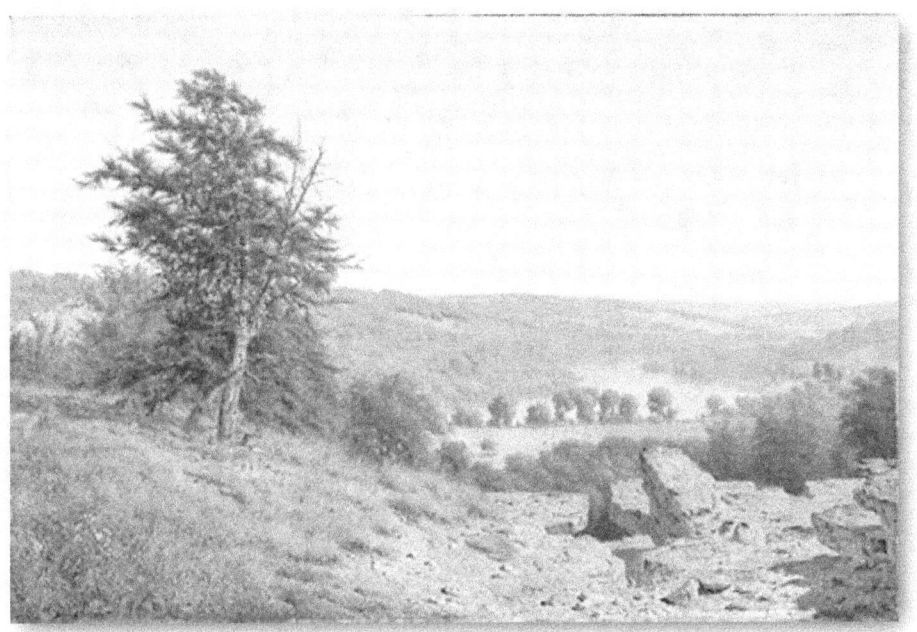

Figure 10. Alexander Helwig Wyant, *Landscape*, 1865. Oil on canvas,
17 1/16 × 25 in. (43.34 × 63.5 cm). Los Angles County Museum of Art,
California. Gift of Joseph T. Mendelson. Accession no. M.66.66.2.

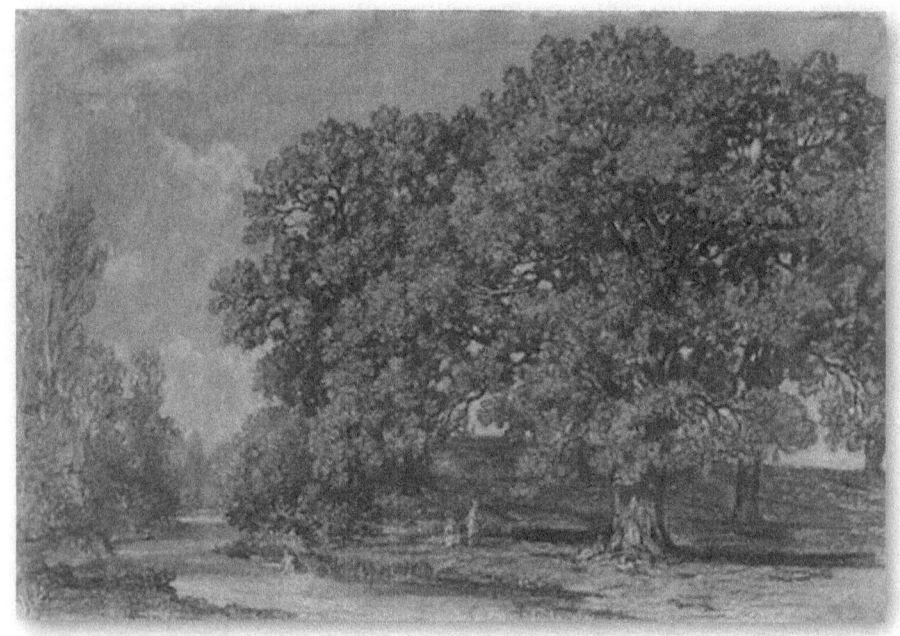

Figure 11. Alexander Helwig Wyant, *Landscape*, YEAR. Charcoal, 11 3/4 × 17 in. (29.85 × 43.18 cm). Los Angeles County Museum of Art, California. Gift of Dr. and Mrs. F. W. Callman. Accession no. 54.84.

BIBLIOGRAPHY

Adorno, Theodor W., and Max Hokheimer. "The Culture Industry: Enlightenment as Mass Deception." In *Stardom and Celebrity: A Reader*, ed. Sean Redmond and Su Holmes, 34–43. London: Sage, 2007.

"American Painters: Alexander H. Wyant, N. A." *Art Journal (1875–1887)*, n.s., 2 (1876): 353–56. http://www.jstor.org/stable/20568990.

"American Painters: Homer D. Martin." *Art Journal (1875–1887)*, n.s., 6 (1880): 321–23. http://jstor.org/stable/20569595.

Andelson, Warren J., David D. Blakelock, and Suysielies M. Blakelock. "Ralph Albert Blakelock." *Ralph Albert Blakelock, 1849–1919*. New York: M. Knoedler, 1973.

"Appreciation in Value of American Paintings." *Brush and Pencil* 14, no. 1 (1904): 14–15. http://www.jstor.org/stable/25540488.

Benjamin, Walter. "The Work of Art in the Age of Mechanical Reproduction." In *Stardom and Celebrity: A Reader*, ed. Sean Redmond and Su Holmes, 35–33. London: Sage, 2007.

Blakelock, Cora. Foreword to *Catalogue of the Works of R .A. Blakelock, N. A., and of His Daughter Marian Blakelock Exhibited at Young's Art Galleries from April 27 to May 13, 1916*, xx–xx. Chicago: Young's Art Galleries, 1916.

Blakelock, David A. "Ralph Albert Blakelock." New York: M. Knoedler,1973.

Boston Evening Transcript. "One of Blakelock's Masterly Nocturnes." February 20, 1917.

Clark, Eliot Candee. *Alexander Wyant.* New York: privately printed, 1916.

Cortissoz, Royal. "Informal Talk by Royal Cortissoz." *Bulletin of the Cleveland Museum of Art* 11, no. 4 (April 1924): 84–86. http://www.jstor.org/stable/25136756.

Davidson, Abraham A. *The Eccentrics and Other American Visionary Painters.* New York: E. P. Dutton, 1978.

Drake, Phillip. "Who Owns Celebrity? Privacy, Publicity and the Legal Regulation of Celebrity Images." In *Stardom and Celebrity: A Reader,* ed. Sean Redmond and Su Holmes, 219–29. London: Sage, 2007.

Dyer, Richard. "Stars." In *Stardom and Celebrity: A Reader,* ed. Sean Redmond and Su Holmes, 78–84. London: Sage, 2007.

"Fake Blakelocks Flood Art Market." *New York Times.* January 20, 1928, 1.

Flexner, James Thomas. *That Wilder Image: The Painting of America's Native School from Thomas Cole to Winslow Homer.* New York: Little, Brown, 1962.

Fulton, Chandos. "A White Mountain Brook." *The Aldine* 6, no. 11 (1873): 218–19. http://www.jstor.org/stable/20636651.

Geske, Norman A. *Beyond Madness: The Art of Ralph Blakelock, 1847–1919.* Lincoln: University of Nebraska Press, 2007.

———. "An Exhibition of Paintings." In *Ralph Albert Blakelock, 1847–1919,* xx–xx. New York: Salander-O'Reilly Galleries, 1987.

Goodrich, Lloyd. "Ralph Albert Blakelock." In *Ralph Albert Blakelock Centenary Exhibition,* xx–xx. New York: Whitney Museum of American Art, 1947.

Graeme, Turner. "The Economy of Celebrity." In *Stardom and Celebrity: A Reader*, ed. Sean Redmond and Su Holmes, 193–205. London: Sage, 2007.

Halasz, Piri. "Art by Blakelock Shown in Trenton." *New York Times*. May 18, 1975, NJ83.

Harrison, Birge. "The Future of American Art." *North American Review* 189, no. 638 (1909): 25–34. http://www.jstor.org/stable/25106273.

Harrison, Helen A. "A Visionary Artist's Output during a Time of Mental Illness." *New York Times*. March 3, 1996.

Isham, Samuel. *The History of American Painting.* New York: Macmillan, 1936.

Jewell, Edward Allen. "100th Anniversary of Blakelock's Birth Is Marked by Exhibition at the Whitney." *New York Times*. April 22, 1947, L116.

Karasoulas, Margarita. *Ralph Albert Blakelock (1847–1919): Iconic Nineteenth-Century American Landscape Painter.* Accessed November 18, 2014. http// www.questroyalfineart.com/artist/ralph-albert-blakelock.

M., F. J. Jr. "An Enigmatic American Landscape." *Record of the Museum of Historic Art, Princeton University* 4, no. 1 (1945): 4. http://www.jstor.org/ stable/3774145.

Mandel, Patricia, C. F. "The Stories behind Three Important Late Homer D. Martin Paintings." *Archives of American Art Journal* 13, no. 3 (1973): 2–8. http://www.jstor.org/stable/1557094.

Martin, Elizabeth Gilbert. *Homer Martin: A Reminiscence, October 28, 1836– February 12, 1897.* New York: William Macbeth, 1904.

Mather, Frank Jewett. *Homer Martin, Poet in Landscape.* New York: Frederic Fairchild Sherman, 1912.

"New York Art." *Brush and Pencil* 5, no. 6 (1900): 270–73. http://www.jstor.org/stable/25505523.

Olpin, Robert. S. "Alexander Helwig Wyant (1836–1892), American Landscape Painter: An Investigation of His Life and Fame and a Critical Analysis of His Work with a Catalogue Raisonné of Wyant Paintings." PhD diss., Boston University, 1971. ProQuest (AAT).

Ravin, James. G. "The Visual Difficulties of Selected Artists and Limitations of Opthalmological Care During the 19th and Early 20th Centuries." *Transactions of the American Ophthalmological Society* 106 (2008): 402–25.

Skalet, Linda. "Thomas B. Clarke, American Collector." *Archives of American Art Journal* 15, no. 3 (1975): 52–83. http://www.jstor.org/stable/1557068.

Smith, Roberta. "Art: The Landscapes of Ralph A. Blakelock." *New York Times*. September 11, 1987, C26.

———. "Islands of Peace in a Life Awash in Sadness." *New York Times*. March 17, 1996, H45.

Spanierman Gallery. *Ralph Albert Blakelock (1847–1919)*. Accessed November 18, 2014. http://www.spanierman.com/Blakelock,-Ralph-Albert/bio/thumbs/biography.

Swift, Samuel. "Americanism in Art." *Brush and Pencil* 15, no. 1 (1905): 51–53, 55–57. http://www.jstor.org/stable/25503769.

"Two Great Artists: Inness and Wyant." *Fine Arts Journal* 27, no. 4 (October 1912): 673–76. http://www.jstor.org/stable/25587149.

Turner, Graham. *Understanding Celebrity*. London: Sage, 2004. E-book.

Van Dyke, John Charles. *American Painting and Its Tradition*. New York: Charles Schriber's Sons, 1919.

Van Eijk Van Voorthuijsen, A. M. E., ed. *World Collectors Annuary*. Delft, Netherlands: Brouwer, n.d.

Vincent, Glyn. *The Unknown Night: The Genius and Madness of R. A. Blakelock, an American Painter*. New York: Grove, 2003.

www.ingramcontent.com/pod-product-compliance
Lightning Source LLC
Chambersburg PA
CBHW070822180526
45168CB00002B/720